Advanced Taxation (ATX-UK)
(Finance Act 2024)

For June 2025 to March 2026
Examination Sittings

Pocket Notes

British library cataloguing-in-publication data

A catalogue record for this book is available from the British Library.

Published by:
Kaplan Publishing UK
Unit 2 The Business Centre
Molly Millars Lane
Wokingham
Berkshire
RG41 2QZ

ISBN 978-1-83996-722-1

© Kaplan Financial Limited, 2024

Printed and bound in Great Britain.

The text in this material and any others made available by any Kaplan Group company does not amount to advice on a particular matter and should not be taken as such. No reliance should be placed on the content as the basis for any investment or other decision or in connection with any advice given to third parties. Please consult your appropriate professional adviser as necessary. Kaplan Publishing Limited and all other Kaplan group companies expressly disclaim all liability to any person in respect of any losses or other claims, whether direct, indirect, incidental, consequential or otherwise arising in relation to the use of such materials.

All rights reserved. No part of this publication may be reproduced, stored in a retrieval system, or transmitted, in any form or by any means, electronic, mechanical, photocopying, recording or otherwise, without the prior written permission of Kaplan Publishing.

Contents

		Reference to Study text chapter	Page Number
Chapter 1	Corporation tax – liability and losses	1, 3	1
Chapter 2	Groups – corporation tax and VAT	4	31
Chapter 3	Overseas issues – corporation tax and VAT	5, 27	51
Chapter 4	Capital gains tax – introduction	6, 7	67
Chapter 5	Capital gains tax – shares and securities	8	83
Chapter 6	Capital gains tax – reliefs	9	93
Chapter 7	Stamp taxes	6, 8	111
Chapter 8	Inheritance tax	10-12	115
Chapter 9	Trusts	13	145
Chapter 10	Ethics, personal financial management and self-assessment	14, 15, 18	155
Chapter 11	Income tax – overview and investment income	16, 18	187
Chapter 12	Employment income – income tax and national insurance	17	199
Chapter 13	Relief for pensions	19	219
Chapter 14	Personal tax – overseas aspects	12, 20	227

Advanced taxation

	Reference to Study text chapter	Page Number
Chapter 15 Personal tax planning	7, 12, 16, 18	25
Chapter 16 Business tax	21-23	26
Chapter 17 Business finance and tax planning for companies	25, 24	30
Chapter 18 Value added tax	26, 27	32
Index		I

Preface

These pocket notes contain the key points you need to know for the exam, presented in a unique way that makes revision easy and effective.

Written by experienced lecturers and authors, these pocket notes break down content into manageable chunks to maximise your concentration.

Quality and accuracy are of the utmost importance to us so if you spot an error in any of our products, please send an email to mykaplanreporting@kaplan.com with full details, or follow the link to the feedback form in MyKaplan.

Our Quality Co-ordinator will work with our technical team to verify the error and take action to ensure it is corrected in future editions.

The exam

Section A

One compulsory 50-mark question

40 technical marks

10 professional skills marks

The professional skills tested in this question will include communication, analysis and evaluation, scepticism and commercial acumen.

Section B

Two compulsory 25-mark questions

20 technical marks each

5 professional skills marks each

Any professional skill (with the exception of communication) can be tested in section B questions.

The entire syllabus can be tested in either section A or section B.

Candidates will be expected to undertake both calculation and narrative work. The questions will be scenario-based and may involve consideration of more than one tax, some elements of planning and the interaction of taxes.

The examination time is 3 hours and 15 minutes.

The ATX exam is only offered as a computer based exam. The ACCA Practice Platform can be used to practise questions in the exam format.

Topics which are not tested at TX and are new to ATX will be frequently examined. However, candidates will also need a thorough knowledge and understanding of the basic tax rules tested in the TX syllabus.

Exam focus

The examining team has stated that the ATX exam will concentrate on the application of tax rules and will require the demonstration of evaluation and explanation skills.

They will set questions involving:

- the interaction of taxes
- decision making within the facts of a given situation
- making choices in a given situation and evaluating the tax savings which can be made.

Questions in section A will be open ended and are likely to require presentation in the form of a report or letter.

Section B questions will be more structured in their requirements.

Aim of the paper

To apply relevant knowledge and skills and exercise professional judgement in providing relevant information and advice to individuals and businesses on the impact of the major taxes on financial decisions and situations.

Main capabilities

- Understanding of the UK tax system through the study of more advanced topics within the taxes studied previously and the study of stamp taxes (A)
- Impact of relevant taxes on various situations and courses of action, including the interaction of taxes (B)
- Minimising and/or deferring tax liabilities by the use of standard tax planning measures (C)
- Professional skills (D)
- Employability and technology skills (E)

The keys to success: ATX

Master the technical content

- Learn the rules, definitions and pro formas
- Practise questions to improve your ability to apply the techniques and perform the calculations
- Practise writing explanations of the rules to improve your understanding and written skills
- Be prepared to produce a report /letter / memorandum.

Provide advice and exercise judgement

Higher skills

- Express yourself in clear, concise technical language.
- Apply common sense to the problem as well as your technical knowledge.
- Tailor your answer to the facts of the question and make references to the scenario given.
- Be prepared to express an opinion or draw a conclusion from the facts given – if the question asks for an opinion, give one.
- Be prepared to suggest improvements to a proposed strategy and to identify tax planning opportunities.
- When dealing with more than one tax, address each one separately.

chapter 1

Corporation tax – liability and losses

In this chapter

- Accounting periods.
- Taxable total profits computation.
- Corporation tax payable.
- Trading profits – specific issues for companies.
- Capital allowances.
- Long period of account.
- Self-assessment.
- Penalties.
- Trading losses – single company.
- Restriction of carry forward of losses.
- Non-trading losses.

Corporation tax – liability and losses

Exam focus

Corporation tax is very important.

Questions on corporation tax will regularly feature in the examination and you need to be able to prepare a corporation tax computation, as well as explain the tax implications of company transactions.

This chapter revises the key issues in preparing a corporation tax computation, summarises the self-assessment rules and sets out the options for a single company making losses.

Accounting periods (APs)

- Corporation tax computation required for each AP.
- Cannot be longer than 12 months.
- Starts:
  - when start to trade
  - previous AP ends.
- Ends:
  - 12 months after start
  - end of period of account (i.e. company's period for which it prepares accounts)
  - cease to trade/be resident in UK
  - go into administration/liquidation.

Taxable total profits computation

ABC Ltd
Corporation tax computation for year ended 31 March 2025

	Notes	£
Trading profits	(a)	X
Interest income	(b)	X
Overseas income	(c)	X
Property income		X
Net chargeable gains	(d)	X
Total profits		X
Less: QCD relief	(e)	(X)
Taxable total profits (TTP)	(f)	X

Corporation tax payable

- Tax liability:

	Notes	£
TTP × relevant %	(g)	X
Less: Marginal relief (if applicable)	(g)	(X)
Less: DTR		(X)
CT payable		X

Corporation tax – liability and losses

Notes

(a) Trading profit = Adjusted trading profit less capital allowances. Adjustments include interest and royalties paid for trade purposes.

(b) Interest income on non-trading loan relationships (i.e. interest receivable and payable).

(c) Overseas income may include rental income, interest income and branch profits, but excludes overseas dividends.

(d) Net chargeable gains
 = capital gains less all capital losses:
 - Indexation allowance (IA) available up to December 2017, or date of disposal if earlier
 - Indexation factors given in examination
 - cannot create or increase a capital loss
 - no AEA
 - consider rollover relief and substantial shareholding exemption.

(e) Qualifying charitable donations (QCDs)
 - includes all charitable donations by company which are not allowed as a trading expense.

(f) Dividend income from UK and overseas companies is never chargeable to corporation tax and not included in TTP.

 However, is included in augmented profits for instalment and corporation tax rate purposes.

(g) The rate of corporation tax is fixed for each financial year. The rate for FY2022 was 19% for all companies.

 The rates for FY2023 and FY2024 are as follows:
 - 25% for companies with augmented profits > £250,000
 - 19% for companies with augmented profits ≤ £50,000
 - 25% less: Marginal relief for companies with augmented profits between £50,000 and £250,000

The above limits need to be divided by the number of associated companies and should also be time apportioned for a short accounting period.

Marginal relief

Marginal relief is calculated as follows:

(Upper limit − augmented profits) ×

Standard fraction × $\dfrac{\text{Taxable total profits}}{\text{Augmented profits}}$

Trading profits – specific issues for companies

- Loan relationships
- Goodwill and other intangibles
- Research and development
- Gains on shares of companies

Loan relationships

All income, expenses, capital and revenue arising from loans is taxed under the loan relationship rules.

	Trading loan	**Non-trading loan**
Example	Loan notes issued to raise funds to acquire P&M	Loan to acquire investment property or a subsidiary
Income/ capital profit	Trading income	Interest income
Expense/ capital loss	Deduct from trading income	Deduct from interest income. Relief available for net loss

Exam focus

Exam kit questions on this area:

Section B questions

- Kitz Ltd

Corporation tax – liability and losses

Goodwill and other intangibles

Intangibles (excluding goodwill)

- Intangible assets acquired by companies are not capital assets for capital gains purposes, but follow accounting treatment.
- Debits and credits, income and capital = part of trading income assessment.
- A company can claim a 4% WDA p.a. if no amortisation in financial accounts or amortisation rate is < 4% p.a.
- On sale of intangibles:
  - profit or loss is taxable/deductible for trading purposes.
- Accounting profit or loss will give rise to an identical tax profit or loss:
  - unless the 4% election is made
  - in which case a tax adjustment must be made by comparing the accounting profit to the taxable profit.

Goodwill

- The treatment of goodwill differs from other intangible assets.
- Amortisation or impairments of goodwill are disallowable for corporation tax.
- Profit/loss on disposal = proceeds less cost (as book value for tax = cost)
  - Profit on disposal = taxable as part of trading profits
  - Loss on disposal = relieved as a non-trading debit.

Special intangibles rollover relief

- If a new intangible is acquired:
  - within 12 months before or up to 36 months after
  - part of the taxable credit may be deferred.
- Applies to goodwill and other intangibles

- Maximum deferral is:

	£
Lower of:	
– Proceeds	
– Amount reinvested	X
Less: Cost of original intangible	(X)
	X

Exam focus

Exam kit questions on this area:

Section A questions
- Janus plc Group
- Mita and Snowdon
- Joe and Fiona

Section B questions
- Maria and Granada Ltd
- Achiote Ltd
- Kitz Ltd
- Evora Ltd

Research and development expenditure (R&D)

- Expenditure on R&D as defined by GAAP qualifies for research and development expenditure credit (RDEC) for companies.
- Expenditure includes:
  - Staffing costs (including NICs, pension costs)
  - Agency staff
  - Materials, water, fuel and power
  - Software
  - Data and cloud computing services
  - 65% of payments to subcontractors (unless connected)
- Expenditure excludes:
  - Taxable benefits
  - Rent

RDEC

- 20% × qualifying revenue expenditure is:
  - included as taxable trading profit, and
  - deducted from CT liability.
- If insufficient CT liability, excess tax credit may be:
  - carried forward, or
  - group relieved, or
  - paid in cash.

Capital expenditure on R&D

- Qualifies for 100% FYA.
- Does not qualify for RDEC.

Exam focus

Exam kit questions on this area:

Section A questions

- Mita and Snowdon

Section B questions

- Dent Ltd
- Damiana plc
- Sabin and Patan Ltd

Gains on shares for companies

Substantial shareholding exemption

- Disposal of shares out of a substantial shareholding (SSE) in a trading company = exempt from corporation tax.
- Substantial shareholding = where company has owned:
  - ≥ 10% interest in the shares
  - for ≥ 12 months continuously
  - in the last 6 years.
- If shares held < 12 months exemption still applies if:
  - shares disposed of are in a new company, and
  - trade and assets of another 75% group company are transferred to that new company prior to sale of shares, and
  - trade and assets have been owned by group for ≥ 12 months in last 6 years.

Exam focus

Exam kit questions on this area:

Section A questions

- Janus plc Group
- Sprint Ltd and Iron Ltd
- Gail and Brad
- Grand Ltd Group

Section B questions

- Acryl Ltd and Cresco Ltd
- Achiote Ltd
- Kitz Ltd

If SSE does not apply

Gains on shares for companies

- If disposal not out of a substantial shareholding:
  - use matching rules for companies, and
  - calculate a gain.
- The matching rules for company disposal of shares are:
  - Same day acquisitions
  - Acquisitions in the previous nine days (FIFO basis)
  - Acquisitions from the share pool.
- Calculation of gains
  - No IA given on same day acquisitions and purchases in previous 9 days
  - IA is available on share pool shares.

The share pool

The share pool for companies is different to the share pool for individuals as follows:

- It contains shares in the same company of the same class, purchased up to 9 days before the date of disposal.
- The pool keeps a record of the:
  - number of shares acquired and sold
  - cost of the shares, and
  - indexed cost of the shares (i.e. cost plus indexation allowance).
- The pool cost and the indexed cost will be provided in the examination.
- When shares are disposed of out of the share pool, the appropriate proportion of the cost and indexed cost which relates to the shares disposed of is calculated on an average cost basis (as for individuals).

Capital allowances

Capital allowances apply to companies in the same way as unincorporated businesses (Chapter 16), with the following additional points:

(1) The AIA must be split between related companies.

   Companies owned by the same individual will be regarded as related where they:
   - are engaged in the same activities,
   - or share the same premises.

   In such circumstances the owner of the companies can choose how to allocate a single AIA between them.

   This could be the case if an individual runs two companies from home, the AIA will be split between the two businesses. Unrelated companies owned by the same individual will each be entitled to the full AIA.

(2) For capital allowance purposes, only one AIA is available to a group of companies.

   Note that:
   - A 'group' for this purpose is defined by the Companies Act and essentially applies where a parent company holds a simple majority shareholding (> 50%) in another company or companies at the end of the accounting period.

   When allocating the AIA:
   - the group members can allocate the maximum £1,000,000 AIA in any way across the group
   - the AIA does not have to be divided equally between them

- all of the allowance can be given to one company, or any amount can be given to any number of companies within the group.

(3) The 6% special rate of WDA in respect of plant and machinery that is integral to a building applies to both initial and replacement expenditure.

Replacement expenditure occurs where more than 50% of an asset is replaced in a 12-month period.

This prevents a tax deduction being claimed for the repair of such assets where such repairs are substantial and the asset can be used in the trade.

Previously, a deduction was allowed for repairs expenditure, on an asset if it could be used in the trade before the 'repairs' were carried out.

This deduction is not available for plant and machinery integral to a building; instead tax relief is spread via the special rate WDA.

(4) There are no private use adjustments for companies, so there are no private use asset columns.

(5) Companies are able to claim enhanced capital allowances for qualifying plant and machinery (details below)

Enhanced capital allowances (ECAs)

Companies purchasing **new** plant and machinery from 1 April 2023 can claim:

- **full expensing: 100% first year allowance (FYA)** for main pool assets
- **50% FYA** for special rate pool assets

ECAs are not available on:

- Second-hand assets
- Cars
- Connected party transactions
- Assets bought in the final period of trading

The AIA should be claimed before ECAs against:

(1) Second-hand special rate pool assets
(2) Second-hand main pool assets
(3) New special rate pool assets (before 50% FYA)
(4) New main pool assets (before full expense 100% FYA)

Disposals of assets on which ECAs were claimed

Disposals of assets that qualified for the 130% super deduction, or full expensing, will trigger an immediate balancing charge equal to the disposal proceeds.

Disposals of assets that qualified for the 50% FYA will trigger an immediate balancing charge calculated as:

- proceeds × proportion of expenditure on which FYA claimed × 50%

The remaining proceeds are deducted from the balance on the special rate pool before calculating the 6% WDA.

Exam focus

Exam kit questions on this area:

Section A questions

- Joe and Fiona
- Waverley and Set Ltd Group
- Plad Ltd and Quil Ltd

Capital allowances pro forma for companies

	AIA	FYA	Full expense	Main pool	SRP	SLA	Allowance
	£	£	£	£	£	£	£
TWDV b/f				X	X	X	
Additions: No AIA/FYA (Cars)				X	X		
Additions: with AIA							
Second-hand SRP additions	X						
AIA (Max £1,000,000 in total)	(X)						X
					X		
Second-hand MP additions	X						
AIA (Max £1,000,000 in total)	(X)						X
				X			
New SRP additions	X						
AIA (Max £1,000,000 in total)	(X)						X
SRP balance for 50% FYA		X					
New MP additions	X						
AIA (Max £1,000,000 in total)	(X)						X
MP balance for full expensing			X				
Full expensing			(X)				X

Chapter 1

(Continued)	AIA	FYA	Full expense	Main pool	SRP	SLA	Allowances
Disposals							
Lower of cost & proceeds				(X)	(X)	(X)	
BC on assets qualifying for super deduction/full expensing							(X)
BC on proceeds relating to 50% FYA							(X)
Remaining proceeds re 50% FYA					(X)		
				X	X	X	
BA/BC						(X)/X	X/(X)
Small pool WDA (if applicable)							
WDA @ 18%				(X)			X
WDA @ 6%					(X)		X
Additions: With FYA							
SRP additions with FYA @ 50%		(X)					X
					X		
Zero-emission cars		X					
FYA @ 100%		(X)					X
				0			
TWDV c/f				X	X		
Total allowances							X

Structures and buildings allowances (SBAs)

Available for qualifying costs of new non-residential structures and buildings, and subsequent renovations or extensions of existing buildings.

- Non-qualifying = costs of land, legal fees, stamp duty land tax or repairs.

SBAs available:

- 3% straight line
- from date brought into use
- time apportion if part way through AP.

On disposal:

- seller time apportions SBAs to date of disposal
- no balancing allowance or balancing charge
- sale proceeds for calculation of gain = increased by SBAs claimed
- buyer receives remainder of SBAs at 3% based on original cost.

Exam focus

Exam kit questions on this area:

Section A questions
- Janus plc Group
- Plad Ltd and Quil Ltd

Section B questions
- Sabin and Patan Ltd
- Rabo Ltd
- Yaqui

Long period of account

Accounting period > 12 months must be split into two APs:
- First 12 months
- Remainder

For each AP, HMRC requires:
- a separate CT comp, and
- a separate CT600 return.

Note there will be:
- Two separate pay days
 (i.e. 9 months and 1 day after end of AP)
- But only one file date of the returns
 (i.e. 12 months after end of long period of account).

Corporation tax – liability and losses

Splitting the profits:

Tax adjusted trading profit before capital allowances	Time-apportion
Capital allowances	Separate computations (where the computation is less than 12 months, the WDA/AIA is reduced accordingly but not FYA)
Interest/Property/Other income	Calculate accrued amount for each period separately (Note)
Chargeable gains	According to date of disposal
Qualifying charitable donations	According to date paid

Note: if information to apply the strict accruals basis is not available, then time apportion.

Self-assessment

Payment date
• Normal date
• Large company (below)
	• 9 months and 1 day after end of AP
	• 4 quarterly instalments:
	on 14th of months 7, 10, 13 and 16 after start of AP
	• Based on estimated liability for the year
	• Payments must be reviewed and revised as necessary at each instalment date
	• A company will not be required to make quarterly instalments in two circumstances:
	  (1) CT liability < £10,000
	  (2) Company not large in previous AP, and augmented profits ≤ £10 million (÷ number of associated companies at the end of the previous period and/or reduced for short AP)

Payment method	• Payment must be made electronically
Filing date	• 12 months after end of period of account • Must be filed electronically along with copies of accounts • Must be filed using Inline eXtensible Business Reporting Language (iXBRL)

Corporation tax – liability and losses

Late payment interest / Repayment interest	<ul><li>Charged from due date</li><li>Earned from date paid</li><li>Charges and receipts are interest income/expense under the loan relationship rules</li></ul>
Retention of records	<ul><li>6 years from end of AP</li></ul>
Group payment arrangements	<ul><li>Optional</li><li>Where at least one group company pays instalments</li><li>Associated companies can arrange for one group company to pay quarterly instalments on behalf of group</li><li>Can save interest as overpayments effectively netted off against underpayments</li><li>Each company must still prepare separate corporation tax computation at end of AP</li></ul>

Large companies

- Large companies must pay corporation tax by instalments (per table above).
- A company is large if its augmented profits for the AP > £1.5 million threshold:
  - short AP – time apportion threshold
  - Associated companies – divide by total number of related companies at end of previous AP.

Augmented profits

	£
TTP	X
Dividends received	X
Augmented profits	X

- Exclude dividends from associated companies

Exam focus

Exam kit questions on this area:

Section A questions

- Waverley and Set Ltd Group

Compliance checks

- HMRC must give written notice of its intention to commence a compliance check (enquiry) into a tax return.
- The time limit to make a compliance check:

  Where a return is submitted on time:
  - 12 months after the actual submission date.

  Where a return is submitted late:
  - 12 months after 31 January, 30 April, 31 July or 31 October following the actual filing date of the return.
- A compliance check ends when HMRC gives notice.
- Company has 30 days to amend the return, if applicable.

Amendments, errors and mistakes

- A company may amend its return:
  - within 12 months from the filing date
- HMRC may amend a return:
  - within 9 months from the date the return is filed.
- A company may make a claim for overpayment relief:
  - within four years from the end of the relevant accounting period.

Penalties

Standard penalties
- Same rules for income tax, corporation tax, CGT, VAT and NIC (Chapter 10).

Other penalties for corporation tax

Offence	Penalty
Failure to keep and retain required records.	Up to £3,000 per accounting period.
Late filing of corporation tax return: • Within 3 months of filing date • More than 3 months after filing date Additional penalties: • 6-12 months after filing date • More than 12 months after filing date	• Fixed penalty = £100 (Note) • Fixed penalty increased to £200 (Note) • Additional 10% of tax outstanding 6 months after filing date • Additonal penalty increased to 20% Note: Fixed penalties rise to £500 and £1,000 if persistently filed late (i.e. return for 2 preceding periods also late)

Trading losses – single company

Summary of reliefs

Carry forward relief	Current year relief	Carry back relief
		Current year offset first then carry back 12 months
<ul><li>Offset against:<ul><li>Total profits (income and gains)</li><li>Before QCD relief</li></ul></li><li>Optional claim</li><li>Partial claims possible</li><li>Indefinite carry forward</li></ul>	<ul><li>Offset against<ul><li>Total profits (income and gains)</li><li>Before QCD relief</li></ul></li><li>Carry forward any remaining losses</li><li>Must offset maximum amount possible if claimed</li><li>QCD relief is lost if no profits to offset against</li><li>Optional claim</li></ul>	

Trading loss pro forma

	2023 £	2024 £	2025 £
Trading profit	X	0	X
Other income	X	X	X
Net chargeable gains	X	X	X
Total profits	X	X	X
Less: Loss relief			
– Current year		(X)1	
– Carry back	(X)2		
– Carry forward			(X)3
	0	0	X
Less: QCD relief	Wasted	Wasted	(X)
Taxable total profits	0	0	X

Key Point

2024 is the loss-making year. The trading profit assessment in this year is £Nil.

Keep a separate working of the loss and how it is utilised.

Assuming there is sufficient loss available, and assuming that the loss is being relieved as early as possible, the order in which to offset the loss is as follows:

(1) Current year relief; in the year the loss is made.

(2) Prior year relief; carrying available losses for offset back 12 months.

(3) Future year relief; against total profits with no need to waste QCDs.

Exam focus

Use the loss pro forma to help you adopt a methodical approach to a question involving trading losses.

Show your workings in a loss working summarising how the loss has been offset.

Approach to loss offset

(1) Lay out years – columnar form.
(2) Calculate TTP ignoring losses.
(3) Choose loss relief by reference to:
    - tax saving:
        - aim to save tax at highest possible rate
        - corporation tax rates are based on the level of augmented profits of the company
    - cash flow:
        - carry back may result in a repayment of tax
        - carry forward will only result in a reduction of future tax
    - offset as soon as possible
    - wastage of QCDs:
        - unrelieved QCDs cannot be carried foward.
(4) Use separate loss working.
(5) If more than one loss, deal with earliest first.

Exam focus

Exam kit questions on this area:

Section A questions
- Drench, Paprikash, Hail Ltd and Rain Ltd
- Janus plc Group
- Plad Ltd and Quil Ltd

Section B questions
- Fox Ltd

Terminal loss relief

- Loss in final 12 months of trading:
  - current year offset; then
  - carryback against total profits (before QCD relief)
  - of 3 years preceding loss-making period
  - on a LIFO basis.

Exam focus

Exam kit questions on this area:

Section B questions

- Acryl Ltd and Cresco Ltd

Restriction of carry forward of losses

- Where the trade becomes small or negligible losses can only be carried forward against trading profits arising from the same trade.
- If the trade ceases losses cannot be carried forward.
- Cannot carry forward losses beyond the date of a change in ownership (> 50% shares) where:
  - a negligible trading activity is revived after a change in ownership, or
  - change in ownership and a major change in the nature of trade in a 5 year period.

Exam focus

Exam kit questions on this area:

Section B questions

- Maria and Granada Ltd
- Rabo Ltd

Non-trading losses

NON-TRADING LOSSES

CAPITAL LOSSES

- Current year then carry forward
- Against chargeable gains only

- Partial claims are not allowed
- Losses must be offset as soon as possible

PROPERTY INCOME LOSSES

- Current year then carry forward
- Against total profits before QCD relief

- Partial claims only allowed for losses carried forward

LOAN RELATIONSHIP DEFICITS

Four options available:
- against total profits before QCD relief of the current period
- carry back against interest income of the previous 12 months
- carry forward against total profits before QCD relief of future periods
- group relief

- Partial claims are allowed
- The company can therefore choose how much of the deficit is relieved under each option
- Claims for current period and carry back relief must be made within two years of the end of the AP of loss

Corporation tax – liability and losses

chapter 2

Groups – corporation tax and value added tax

In this chapter

- Group relationships.
- Group relief.
- Consortium relief.
- Capital gains groups.
- Sale of shares or assets.
- Transfer of trade within 75% group.
- Transfer pricing.

Groups – corporation tax and value added tax

Exam focus

Questions on groups can be examined in the A or B section of the exam.

There has been a large corporation tax groups scenario on almost every ATX examination so far.

Group relationships

Relationship	Definition
Associated companies	• One company controls (> 50%) another, or • Both are controlled by the same person.
Group relief (GR) group	• A parent company and all its direct and indirect 75% subsidiaries (later in this chapter). • The definition of 75% subsidiary is extended for GR purposes only. In addition to owning 75% of the share capital (SC) the parent must also be entitled to receive 75% of profits and 75% of assets on winding up.
Capital gains group	• A parent company (principal member (PM)) and its 75% subsidiaries (later in this chapter) and their 75% subsidiaries – provided PM has > 50% effective interest in subsidiary. • A 75% subsidiary of a PM cannot be a PM itself (i.e. a company can only be a member of one gains group).
75% subsidiary	• One company owns ≥ 75% of SC of another, or • Both are 75% subsidiaries of a third company. • Includes direct/indirect holdings. • Definition includes overseas companies.

Groups – corporation tax and value added tax

Relationship	Definition
Consortium owned company	• ≥ 75% ordinary SC owned by companies, each owning ≥ 5% and • Each member entitled to ≥ 5% profits and ≥ 5% net assets • Excludes a company that is 75% subsidiary of another.

Illustration – Group relationships

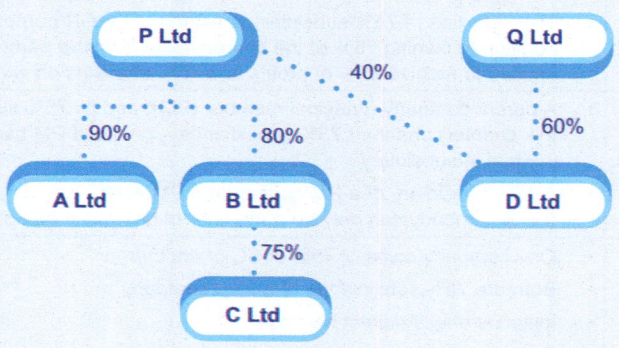

Relationship	Group members
Associated companies of P Ltd	• A Ltd, B Ltd and C Ltd • D Ltd excluded as < 50%
Group relief (GR) group	• P Ltd, A Ltd, B Ltd • C Ltd is not part of the group as P Ltd's interest is < 75% i.e. interest in C Ltd = 60% (80% × 75%) • B Ltd and C Ltd form a separate losses group
Capital gains group	• P Ltd, A Ltd, B Ltd and C Ltd • C Ltd is part of the gains group as it is a 75% subsidiary of a 75% subsidiary and P Ltd's effective interest (60%) is > 50%
Consortium relief group	• D Ltd is a consortium company of P Ltd and Q Ltd • D Ltd is owned ≥ 75% by companies and each consortium member (P Ltd and Q Ltd) is entitled to ≥ 5%

Key Point

You must be clear on the distinction between a group relief group and a capital gains group.

Groups – corporation tax and value added tax

- Associated companies include:
  - Both UK and overseas resident companies
  - Companies leaving group.
- Exclude:
  - Dormant companies
  - Non-trading holding company

Effect of associated companies:

Effect:

- Divide the threshold by the number of associated companies to determine whether instalments are necessary.
- Dividends from associated companies (UK and overseas) = not included in augmented profit.
- Divide the upper and lower limits by the number of associated companies to determine the relevant rate of corporation tax.
- One AIA allocated between associated companies.
- VAT group registration available.
- Group payment arrangement available at least one company pays by quarterly instalments.

Key Point

Note that:

- The number of associated companies is based on the position at the end of the previous AP when determining whether instalments are necessary. However, when determining the relevant rate of corporation tax, it is necessary to look at the number of associates in the current AP regardless of when they became associated.

Group relief (GR)

- Transfer losses between any member of a GR group.
- Group definition:
  - includes overseas companies
  - but the relief can generally only be claimed by UK resident companies.

Exam focus

Exam kit questions on this area:

Section A questions

- Janus plc Group
- Drench, Paprikash, Hail Ltd and Rain Ltd
- Sprint Ltd and Iron Ltd
- Hahn Ltd Group
- Waverley and Set Ltd Group
- Plad Ltd and Quil Ltd

Section B questions

- Rabo Ltd

Groups – corporation tax and value added tax

- Rules:

Surrendering co.	Claimant co.
Any amount of **current year**: – trading loss – debits on non trading loan relationships. Plus **excess**: – QCD relief – UK property losses – expenses of management. Can surrender **brought forward**: – trading losses – NTLR deficits – UK property losses – expenses of management. The surrendering company can only surrender to the extent it cannot use the above against its own total profits.	Maximum claim: £ TTP (a) X Less: CY losses (b) (X) X (a) TTP is after deduction of losses b/f and QCDs. (b) The company's own losses are taken into account in computing the maximum claim, but need not actually be claimed before GR.

- Watch for:
    - non-coterminous APs
        - GR restricted to common AP (profits/losses deemed to accrue evenly).
    - companies joining group
        - GR only available for losses arising whilst in the group
        - Losses arising in a subsidiary before it joins the group are not available for group relief for 5 years after joining.
    - companies leaving group
        - GR only available for losses arising whilst in group, but
        - No GR once arrangements for sale are in place.

Due date for group relief claim

- 12 months after the claimant company's filing date for the AP covered by the claim (i.e. usually 2 years after the end of the AP).

Payment for group relief

- The claimant company may pay the surrendering company for the loss.
- Any such payment for the group relief is ignored in both companies' CT computations.

Consortium relief

- Two or more companies owning:
  - Together ≥ 75% of another company and
  - Individually ≥ 5%
  - No one company owns ≥ 75%
  - UK companies only, but overseas companies can help to meet the definition.
- Similar to group relief but:
  - Losses to surrender:
    - between consortium company (CC) and UK members only (i.e. not between members)
    = lower of:
      - member's TTP / loss
      - (member's % holding in CC) × CC's TTP / loss.

Exam focus

Always consider whether or not any of the companies in the question form a consortium

Exam focus

Exam kit questions on this area:

Section A questions
- Janus plc Group
- Mita and Snowdon

Capital gains groups

1 Transfer of assets within group

- Automatically take place at no gain/no loss (NGNL) regardless of the price paid.
- Transferee company takes over asset at cost plus indexation to date of transfer.
- Degrouping charge where transferee company leaves the gains group still owning the asset, within 6 years of the NGNL transfer
  - calculated as gain that would have arisen, using MV as proceeds, at date of NGNL transfer
  - degrouping charge is added to the consideration received by the vendor company selling the shares in the company leaving the group
  - unlikely to be taxable as company selling the shares is likely to benefit from substantial shareholding exemption on disposal of the shares
  - group ROR not available for a degrouping gain.
- If an asset is transferred on which SBAs have been claimed:
  - The transferor does not add SBAs to disposal proceeds
  - The transferee is treated as if it has always owned the asset and continues to claim SBAs based on the original cost
  - When the asset is subsequently disposed of by the transferee all SBAs claimed by the group are added to the disposal proceeds for the chargeable gain calculation.

Groups – corporation tax and value added tax

Exam focus

Exam kit questions on this area:

Section A questions

- Drench, Paprikash, Hail Ltd and Rain Ltd
- Janus plc Group
- Gail and Brad

Section B questions

- Rabo Ltd

2 Reallocation of gains

- A joint election can be made to reallocate chargeable gains or allowable losses when an asset is sold outside the group.
- The election enables:
  - group chargeable gains and allowable capital losses to be offset
  - thus maximising the use of capital losses.

Key Point

Current year chargeable gains or allowable losses can be transferred, but not brought forward losses.

3 Rollover relief (replacement of business assets)

- For ROR purposes, all companies within a capital gains group are treated as carrying on a single trade
  - gain in one company can be rolled into the acquisition by another group company
  - group ROR not available for a degrouping gain.

Exam focus

Exam kit questions on this area:

Section A questions
- Jeg Ltd Group
- Hum Ltd Group
- Hahn Ltd Group

Section B questions
- Fox Ltd

4 Pre-entry capital losses
- On joining a gains group
  - identify capital losses (realised losses only).
- Can only use against:
  - gains on own assets held at date of joining group
  - gains on new assets acquired from outside group for use in business.
- Can not be used against gains of other group companies.

5 Restriction on trading losses carried forward

If a company joins a gains group and:
- receives a gain from the new group, or
- makes a gain on an asset transferred from the new group
- within five years of changing owners

then any trading loss arising before it joined the group cannot be used against this gain.

6 Intangible assets
- Similar rules exist for transfer of intangible assets between group members (i.e. tax neutral).
- Degrouping charge if transferee company leaves group within 6 years.
- Degrouping charge can be allocated to another group member.

- If SSE applies to the share disposal there will not be a degrouping charge. The asset will remain at its TWDV and tax relief will continue as it would if the company had not left the group.

7 Stamp taxes

- Assets subject to stamp duty and stamp duty land tax can be transferred between group members as an exempt transfer.
- If the transferee company leaves the group within 3 years the duty is payable.

Approach to a groups question

- AIM = to allocate gains and all losses for the benefit of the group.
- The approach (as a general rule) should be as follows:
  (i) Prepare a diagram of the group structure.
  (ii) Determine the number of associated companies, 75% group(s) and consortia.
  (iii) Set up a tabular pro forma for TTP and augmented profits (if relevant). May need to calculate gains, consider ROR and reallocation of gains to calculate TTP.
  Do this **before** dealing with losses.
  (iv) Complete the TTP, separating out any losses to loss memoranda.
  (v) Determine the best use of any qualifying losses.

(vi) Where there are a number of losses in a question, deal with the losses with the most restricted set off first.

(vii) Calculate CT liability on revised TTP.

(viii) Show CT payable and any losses or surpluses to be carried forward.

- Factors to consider:
  - Tax rates
  - Cash flow
  - Wastage of QCDs.

Sale of shares or assets

Sale of shares:

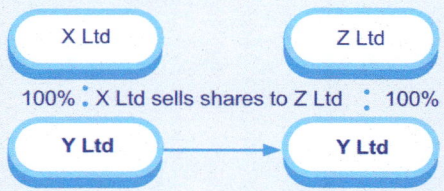

100% : X Ltd sells shares to Z Ltd : 100%

X Ltd
- Gain/loss on disposal of shares unless SSE available.
- Possible degrouping charge: add to disposal proceeds for sale of shares.
- Still include Y Ltd as an associated company in the period of disposal.

Y Ltd
- Carries on trading.
- Group relief stops when arrangements in place: time apportion if mid-year.
- Trading losses c/f may be subject to restriction as Y Ltd has changed owner
- Pre-entry capital losses cannot be used against gains on Z Ltd's assets.
- Associated to X Ltd until the next AP.

Z Ltd
- Associated to Y Ltd in the current AP for the purpose of determining the relevant rate of corporation tax. Associated to Y Ltd from the next AP for the purpose of determining whether instalments are necessary.
- Group relief starts when Y Ltd joins: time apportion if mid-year.
- Pay stamp duty 0.5%.

Exam focus

Exam kit questions on this area:

Section A questions
- Grand Ltd Group

Sale of assets:

Before
- X Ltd
- 100% — Y Ltd sells assets and trade to Z Ltd
- Y Ltd
- L&B P&M Goodwill

After
- Z Ltd
- L&B P&M Goodwill

X Ltd
- No effect.

Y Ltd
- Ceases trading: end of AP.
- Gains/losses on disposal of chargeable assets (e.g. land and buildings).
- Trading profit/loss on disposal of goodwill.
- Possible ROR for gains/profit on goodwill.
- BA/BC on plant and machinery (none for SBAs).
- Losses remain in Y Ltd: possible terminal loss relief.
- VAT: transfer of going concern.

Z Ltd
- Acquires assets at MV.
- Capital allowances for plant and machinery based on MV.
- SBAs based on original cost.
- Pay stamp duty on land and buildings 0 – 5%.

Transfer of trade within a 75% group

SALE OF TRADE AND ASSETS

- **SPECIAL RULES APPLY**
  - **TRADE LOSSES**
    - Can be transferred with the trade
    - Can be used against future total profits
  - **CAPITAL ALLOWANCES**
    - Assets will be transferred at TWDV
    - No BC/BA for transferor
    - No FYA or AIA for transferee
    - SBAs for transferee based on original cost
- **CAPITAL GAINS**
  - **IF GAINS GROUP**
    - Assets pass as usual at NGNL
  - **IF NOT GAINS GROUP**
    - Capital gains/losses will arise on chargeable assets sold

Transfer pricing

- Applies where transactions between group companies, which have not taken place at an arms length price, result in a tax advantage (e.g. decreased profits, increased losses) to a UK company.
- The advantaged company must increase its taxable profits to reflect an arm's length price.
- The other company can reduce its taxable profits by a corresponding amount if it is UK resident.
- Rules only apply where the companies involved are large (or medium sized under limited circumstances).
- Rules do apply if:

  Large → any company
  S/M → overseas company in non-qualifying territory
  (e.g. no DTR agreement).

- Rules do not apply if:

  S/M → UK S/M

  S/M → overseas company in qualifying territory
  (e.g. DTR agreement exists).

Exam focus

Exam kit questions on this area:

Section A questions
- Jeg Ltd Group
- Hahn Ltd Group

Section B questions
- Kitz Ltd
- Achiote Ltd

Groups – corporation tax and value added tax

chapter 3

Overseas issues – corporation tax and value added tax

In this chapter

- Company residence.
- UK company operating overseas.
- Branch exemption election.
- Overseas income – computational approach.
- Controlled foreign companies.
- Overseas aspects of VAT.

Overseas issues – corporation tax and value added tax

Exam focus

Overseas issues are likely to feature as part of a question and are often included within a groups question.

Company residence

Definition

A company is resident in the UK if it is:

- **incorporated** in the UK, or
- incorporated outside the UK and
  - its place of **central management and control** is situated in the UK.

Exam focus

Exam kit questions on this area:

Section B questions

- Spetz Ltd Group

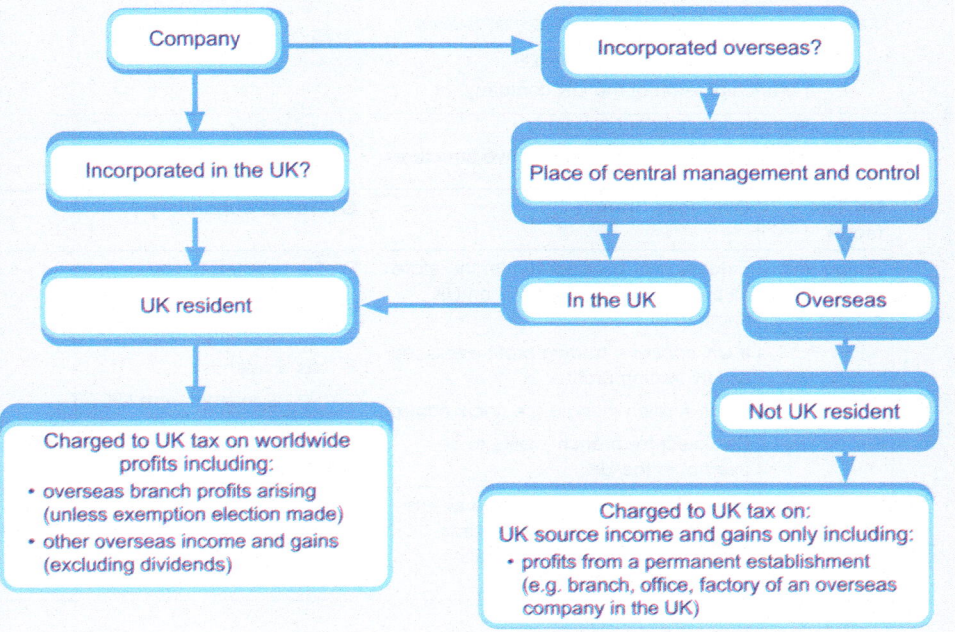

UK company operating overseas

- Can establish operations in 2 ways:
    - a branch/division of the UK company, or
    - an overseas resident subsidiary.
- Different UK tax implications of the two structures.

UK Tax factor	Overseas branch	Overseas subsidiary

Scope and basis of charge	Extension of UK operations; therefore all profits arising assessed on UK company.
	If UK control – trading profit assessed as UK trading profit.
	If not, foreign income (i.e. local control).
	Can elect for branch profits to be exempt in the UK.
		Profits remitted to UK
		• as interest/property income:
		    – is chargeable to UK CT
		• as dividends:
		    – is exempt from UK CT

Capital allowances	Available on overseas located assets purchased and used by overseas branch unless election for branch exemption made.	Not available under UK tax rules.

UK Tax factor (contd)	Overseas branch (contd)	Overseas subsidiary (contd)
Trading loss relief	Can relieve trading losses against UK profits. No relief if election for branch exemption made. Can use UK losses against profits of overseas branch.	No UK trading loss can be surrendered to overseas subsidiary.
Chargeable gains	Capital gains computed using UK rules (i.e. ROR is available on reinvestment and capital losses can be utilised).	UK rules not applicable.

Impact on tax payment dates	None – as **not** a separate entity.	Associated company:
		• Reduces the threshold for determining whether instalments are required.
		• If dividend received from overseas associated company
		  = ignored for augmented profits.
		• If dividend received from overseas non-associated company
		  = included in augmented profits.

Overseas issues – corporation tax and value added tax

Exam focus

Exam kit questions on this area:

Section A questions
- Hum Ltd Group
- Janus plc Group

Section B questions
- Spetz Ltd Group
- Evora Ltd

Branch exemption election

- Can be made at any time
- Effective from start of AP after election made
- Irrevocable
- Applies to all overseas branches

Effect

- Profits = exempt in UK
- Losses = no relief in UK
- No capital allowances
- Capital gains = not taxable in UK

Tax planning

- May be beneficial not to make election if:
    (i) DTR means little or no UK CT payable, and/or
    (ii) losses possible or anticipated in an overseas branch in the future.

Exam focus

Exam kit questions on this area:

Section A questions
- Jeg Ltd Group

Section B questions
- Spetz Ltd Group
- Evora Ltd

Overseas income – computational approach

(1) Calculate the gross amount of overseas income for inclusion in computation of TTP.

	£
Foreign income received	A
Add: WHT = $A \times \dfrac{\% \text{ WHT}}{100 - \% \text{WHT}}$	X
	X

(2) Compute the CT liability on the TTP.

(3) Offset DTR

For each source of overseas income lower of:

- overseas tax suffered, and
- UK tax on overseas income.

(4) Unrelieved overseas tax on branch profits only

Relief may be available via:

- carry back
- carry forward.

Key Point

Offset QCD relief and losses against UK income to maximise DTR.

Exam focus

Exam kit questions on this area:

Section A questions
- Janus plc Group
- Plad Ltd and Quil Ltd
- Jeg Ltd Group
- Hum Ltd Group

Section B questions
- Spetz Ltd Group

Controlled foreign companies (CFCs)

Exam focus

Always consider the possibility of an overseas company being a CFC.

- Provisions exist to prevent UK companies setting up overseas subsidiaries and accumulating profits in countries with lower rates of tax.
- If an overseas company is a CFC, a UK corporate shareholder may be subject to a corporation tax charge (the CFC charge) based on its share in the CFC.

No CFC charge
- CFC charge does not arise if
  - an exemption applies
  - no chargeable profits of CFC
  - the shareholder = an individual.

Key Point

The usual rule of taxing only non-dividend income from an overseas subsidiary and exempting dividend income does not apply to a CFC.

Definition

A non-UK resident company:

- Controlled by UK resident companies, and/or individuals
- that has artificially diverted profits from the UK.

Exemptions to CFC charge

- CFC may have chargeable profits, but no CFC charge as it satisfies one of the exemptions:

Exempt period	The first 12 months of the company coming under the control of UK residents.
Excluded territories	HMRC provide a list of approved territories where rates of tax are sufficiently high to avoid a CFC charge arising.
Low profits	The CFC's TTPs are: • ≤ £500,000 in a 12-month period – of which ≤ £50,000 comprises non-trading profits.
Low profit margin	The CFC's accounting profits are ≤ 10% of relevant operating expenditure.
Tax exemption	The tax paid in the overseas country is ≥ 75% of the UK CT which would be due if it were a UK resident company.

No chargeable profits of CFC

- **Chargeable profits** = income of CFC (not chargeable gains) that are artificially diverted from the UK, calculated using the UK tax rules.
- CFCs = regarded as having **no chargeable profits** (and therefore no CFC charge) if:
  - the CFC does not hold assets or bear any risks
    - that are managed in the UK, or are
    - under tax schemes intended to reduce UK tax, or
  - the CFC would continue in business if the UK management of its assets and risks were to cease.

CFC charge to UK corporation tax

- A CFC charge applies if:
  - **UK company owns ≥ 25%** interest in the CFC
  - the CFC has chargeable profits.
- CFC charge is:

	£
(UK company's share of CFC profits × 25% of CT) (Note)	X
Less: Creditable tax	
DTR that would be available if CFC were UK resident	(X)
CFC charge	X

Note: UK company's share of CFC profits

= **apportioned based on the % of shares held**

- UK companies self-assess their liability to the CFC charge.
- A clearance procedure exists to check how the rules will be applied.

Exam focus

Exam kit questions on this area:

Section A questions

- Waverley and Set Ltd Group

Section B questions

- Klubb plc

Overseas aspects of VAT

VAT on exports
Goods sold to customers outside the UK will be zero-rated supplies.

VAT on imports
Postponed accounting is used for imports as follows:

- Output VAT is recorded on the VAT return covering date of importation
- This is recovered as input VAT (subject to normal rules).

Key Point

All supplies of goods outside the UK = taxable supplies.

Net effect on purchases from within or outside the UK = same, unless purchaser makes exempt supplies.

Supply of services

VAT is generally charged in the place of supply.

Supply of services to	Place of supply
Business customer	Where the customer is established
Non-business customer	Where the supplier is established

Overseas issues – corporation tax and value added tax

These rules can be applied to a UK business as follows:

UK business		Accounting for VAT
Supplies services to	• Overseas business customer (B2B)	• Place of supply is overseas. • Outside the scope of UK VAT.
	• Overseas non-business customer (B2C)	• Place of supply is UK. • Output VAT charged at standard UK rate.

Receives services from	• Overseas business (B2B)	• Place of supply is UK.
		• Reverse charge procedure:
		  – UK business accounts for 'output VAT' at standard UK rate on VAT return.
		  – This VAT can then be reclaimed as input VAT.

Time of supply for cross border supply of services

- For single supplies:
  - tax point = earlier of
    - (i) when the service is completed, or
    - (ii) paid for
- For continuous supplies:
  - tax point = end of each billing or payment period

Exam focus

Exam kit questions on this area:

Section A questions
- Jeg Ltd Group
- Janus plc Group
- Waverley and Set Ltd Group

Section B questions
- Meg and Laurie
- Evora Ltd

Overseas issues – corporation tax and value added tax

chapter 4

Capital gains tax – introduction

In this chapter

- Scope of CGT.
- CGT computation procedure – individuals.
- Pro forma CGT computation.
- Chargeable gain computation – individuals.
- Part disposals.
- Chattels.
- Assignment of leases.
- Assets lost or destroyed.
- Asset damaged.
- Capital losses.
- Connected persons.
- Married couples and civil partners.

Capital gains tax – introduction

Exam focus

Evaluation of capital gains and losses is likely to feature heavily in the examination.

Questions are likely to feature both computational and planning aspects.

This chapter provides the tools to enable you to deal with the computational aspects of different scenarios.

Scope of CGT

- A chargeable gain arises when:
  - a chargeable disposal is made
  - by a chargeable person
  - of a chargeable asset.
- Companies
  - pay corporation tax.
- Individuals
  - pay capital gains tax.

Scope of CGT

Chargeable persons
- individual
- company
- trustee
- partners in a partnership

Chargeable assets
- all assets unless specifically exempt

Chargeable disposals
- sale/gift of whole/part of asset
- loss/destruction of asset
- compensation for damage
- capital sums received re surrender of rights

Exempt assets
- gains – no CGT
- losses – no relief
- examples:
  - qualifying corporate bonds (QCBs) owned by individuals
  - gilts
  - trading inventory
  - receivables
  - equity ISA investments
  - cash
  - endowment policy proceeds
  - cars
  - wasting chattels (e.g. horses, boats)
  - shares in VCT

Exempt disposals
- trading disposal
- transfers on death
- gifts to charity

Capital gains tax – introduction

CGT computation procedure – individuals

Compute the CGT payable by an individual for a tax year as follows:

(1) Calculate the chargeable gains / allowable losses on the disposal of each chargeable asset separately

(2) Consider availability of any CGT reliefs (Chapter 6)

(3) Calculate the net chargeable gains arising in the tax year

= (chargeable gains less allowable losses)

(4) Deduct the annual exempt amount (AEA) = taxable gains

(5) Deduct capital losses brought forward

(6) Calculate the CGT payable at 10% and/or 20% depending on the availability of business asset disposal relief (BADR) or investors' relief (IR), and level of taxable income (18%/24% for residential property)

(7) Deduct tax already paid on UK resident property disposals.

Pro forma CGT computation

	£
Net chargeable gains for tax year (after specific reliefs)	X
Less: AEA (2024/25)	(3,000)
	X
Less: Capital losses b/f	(X)
Taxable gains	X
CGT liability (at appropriate rate)	X
Less: Tax paid on UK residential property	(X)
CGT payable	X

Due date 31 January 2026
(31 January after end of tax year)

Chargeable gain computation – individuals

Exam focus

The following pro forma can be used as the basic layout for the computation of the chargeable gain/allowable loss arising on each disposal by an individual.

Elements of the pro forma are computed differently for specific assets (e.g. part disposals). The approach to take for assets with additional rules is shown on the subsequent pages.

	£
Consideration (a), (b)	X
Less: Incidental costs of sale (c)	(X)
Net disposal proceeds	X
Less: Allowable expenditure	
– acquisition cost (d)	(X)
– incidental costs of acquisition (c)	(X)
– enhancement expenditure	(X)
Chargeable gain/loss	X/(X)

If a chargeable gain arises:

Chargeable gain before reliefs	X
Less: CGT reliefs (e)	(X)
Chargeable gain after reliefs	X

If an allowable loss arises:

Deduct any capital losses for the year from chargeable gains and include the net chargeable gains in the pro forma CGT payable computation.

Notes

(a) Disposal proceeds or market value (MV).

(b) Date of disposal:
date of contract/date conditions satisfied for conditional contracts.

(c) Legal expenses, valuation fees, advertising costs, stamp duty, auctioneer's fees.

(d) Cost/MV/probate value.

(e) Gift holdover relief, rollover relief, incorporation relief, PRR and letting relief, EIS/SEIS relief.

(f) The gain is aggregated with other gains and losses and taxed at 10%, or 20% depending on the AEA, BADR/IR and the level of taxable income. (18% or 24% for residential property gains).

(g) For UK residential property, CGT must be paid to HMRC within 60 days of disposal.

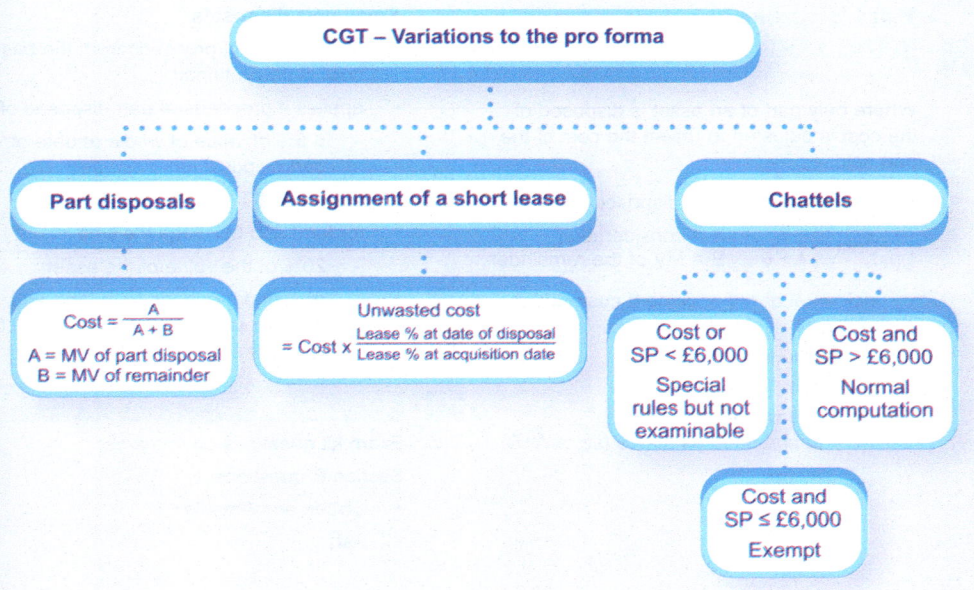

Part disposals

Key Point

Where only part of an asset is disposed of the cost is adjusted to reflect the cost of the part sold.

- Cost of part of asset disposed of:

  $\text{Cost} \times \dfrac{A}{A+B}$ A = consideration
  B = MV of the remainder

- incidental or enhancement costs which relate:
  - wholly to the part sold
    = fully deductible
  - to the whole asset
    = apportioned as above (i.e. A/A+B)

Small part disposals

- elect to deduct proceeds from the base cost of part retained
- applies if proceeds of part disposed of:
  - ≤ 5% of value of whole at date of part disposal, or
  - ≤ £3,000
- for land and buildings the limit is:
  - 20% of the value of the asset,
  - provided proceeds from land and building sales do not exceed £20,000 in the year.

Exam focus

Exam kit questions on this area:

Section B questions

- Caden and Amahle
- Ash

Chattels

> **Definition**

Tangible movable property
(e.g. painting, jewellery, racehorse, boat, caravan).

Wasting chattels:
- expected life ≤ 50 years
  (e.g. racehorse, boat, caravan)
- exempt from CGT unless plant and machinery on which capital allowances available.

Non-wasting chattels:
- expected life > 50 years
  (e.g. antiques, painting)
- subject to £6,000 rule but special rules not examinable.

Assignment of leases

Long lease (i.e. > 50 years)	Short lease (i.e. ≤ 50 years)
• subject to normal CGT computation	• subject to special CGT computation • cost adjusted to reflect depreciating nature of the asset: Allowable cost × $\dfrac{\text{Percentage for remaining life on disposal}}{\text{Percentage for remaining life on acquisition}}$ The % will be provided in the examination

Exam focus

Exam kit questions on this area:

Section B questions:

- Ash
- Samphire Ltd and Kelp Ltd
- Fox Ltd

Assets lost or destroyed

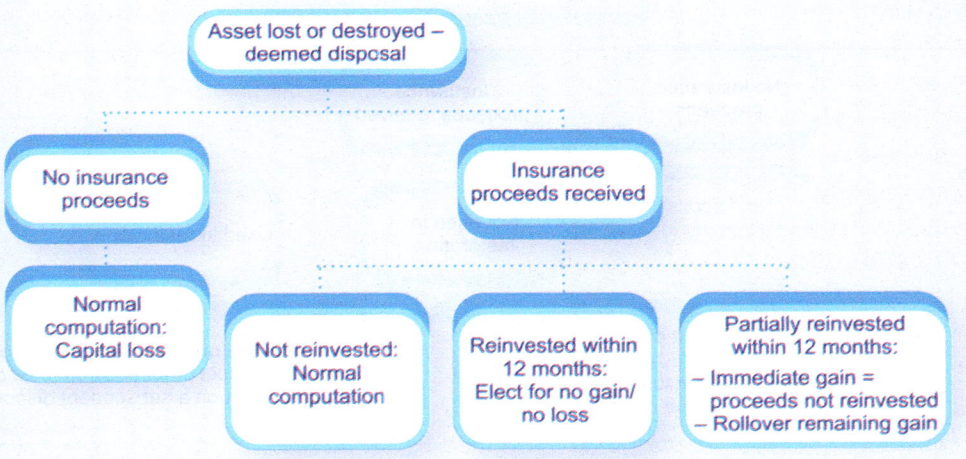

Capital gains tax – introduction

Asset damaged

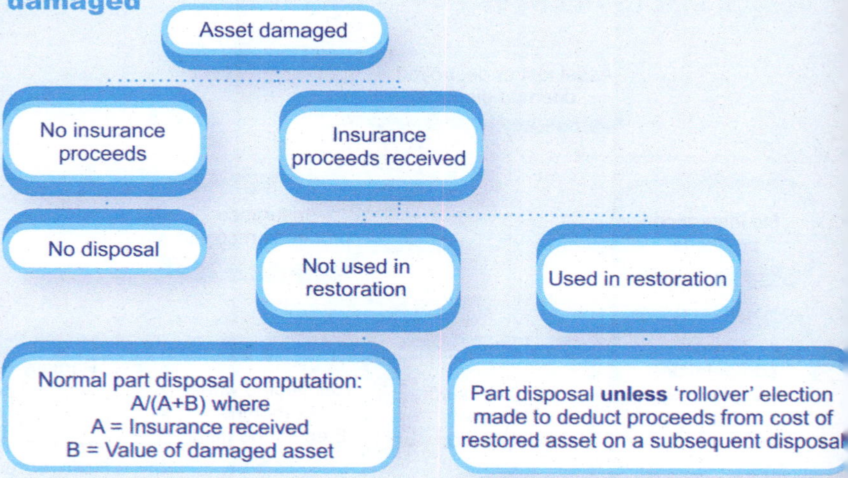

- **Asset damaged**
  - **No insurance proceeds** → No disposal
  - **Insurance proceeds received**
    - **Not used in restoration**: Normal part disposal computation: $A/(A+B)$ where A = Insurance received, B = Value of damaged asset
    - **Used in restoration**: Part disposal **unless** 'rollover' election made to deduct proceeds from cost of restored asset on a subsequent disposal

Exam focus

Exam kit questions in this area:

Section A questions:
- Jake

Section B questions:
- Eric

Capital losses

- Current year losses:
  - must be offset against gains if possible
  - cannot be restricted to preserve the AEA
  - carry forward remaining losses.
- Brought forward losses:
  - offset after the AEA
  - if net chargeable gains after the AEA are £Nil then continue to carry forward.
- Losses in the year of death:
  - can be carried back 3 years
  - LIFO basis
  - can restrict to preserve AEA.

Connected persons

- Consideration for disposal = market value.
- Loss on disposal can only be offset against gains to same connected person.

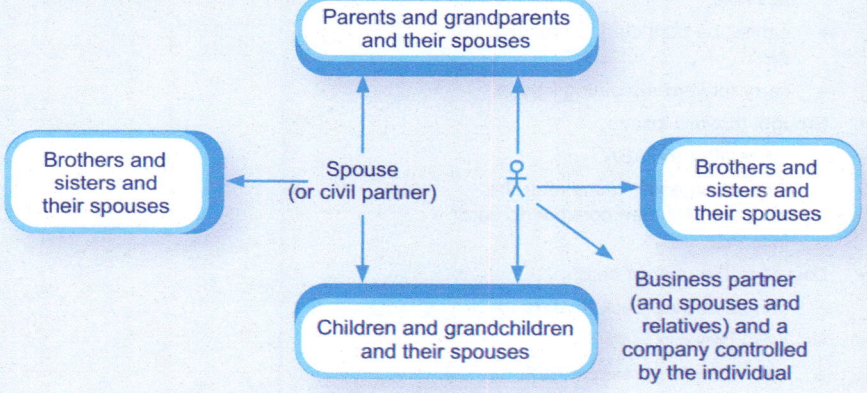

Civil partner and their relatives (as above) are also connected persons.

Exam focus

Exam kit questions on this area:

Section B questions
- Caden and Amahle
- Liber
- Anya
- Traiste Ltd

Capital gains tax – introduction

Married couples and civil partners

Exam focus

Scenarios involving married couples / civil partners are likely to be examined.

It is important that you know how to deal with transactions between spouses / civil partners and also to be able to suggest simple tax planning opportunities to enable them to minimise their total tax liabilities (Chapter 15).

Exam focus

Exam kit questions on this area:

Section A questions

- Ray, Shanira and Kelly

For CGT purposes, spouse / civil partner transfers are treated as follows:

- The connected persons rules are overridden.
- Spouse or civil partner transfers:
  - take place at no gain/no loss
  - regardless of any actual consideration which may have been received.
- These rules only apply until the earlier of
  - the last day of the third tax year following the tax year of separation
  - the date the marriage/civil partnership legally ends/separation is legally recognised.
- The transferor is deemed to dispose of the asset at its acquisition cost
  - i.e. the spouse/civil partner takes over the asset at its original cost.

chapter 5

Capital gains tax – shares and securities

In this chapter

- Share valuation rules.
- Matching rules – individuals.
- The share pool.
- Sale of rights (nil paid).
- Takeovers and mergers.
- QCBs and government securities.
- Liquidations.
- Losses on unquoted shares.

Share valuation rules

Transaction:	Consideration:
Sale	Sale proceeds
Gift	Market value
Transfer to a connected person	Market value

Market value of quoted shares:

Value = the mid-price quoted on the Stock Exchange

- i.e. the average of the lowest and highest prices on the disposal date.

Unquoted shares

- No readily available price – professional valuation required.
- In the exam the value will be given.

Matching rules – individuals

Apply where an individual has made more than one purchase of shares of the same class in the same company.

Disposals matched with:

1. Acquisitions on same day.
2. Acquisitions in the next 30 days (FIFO basis).
3. The share pool (shares acquired before the date of disposal are pooled together

Exam focus

For the ATX examination, a thorough understanding of the basic share identification rules is required.

Disposal of shares by individuals

| Share pool | 30 days |

Date of disposal

Order of matching: (3) (1) (2)

Method to calculate gain:

Step 1 Determine the sale proceeds per share.

Step 2 Identify the date the shares are purchased and using the matching rules allocate the disposal to the time periods above.

Step 3 Calculate the gains / losses arising on each matching rule.

The share pool

- The share pool contains shares in the same company, of the same class, purchased before the date of a disposal.
- It contains the amalgamated cost of shares acquired.
- The cost of shares disposed of is calculated as a proportion of the number of shares removed from the pool.
- Business asset disposal relief (BADR) is available (Chapter 6) on the disposal of shares by an individual provided:
  - the shares are in the individual's personal trading company, and
  - the individual is also an employee of that company.

Capital gains tax – shares and securities

Bonus issues

Definition

Distribution of free shares to shareholders based on their existing shareholding.

For CGT purposes bonus issues are treated as follows:
- The bonus shares are not treated as a separate holding of shares.
- The shares are treated as acquired on the same day as the original shares to which they relate.
- Therefore, the number of bonus shares are included in the share pool but at £Nil cost.

Rights issues

Definition

Offer of new shares to existing shareholders in proportion to their existing shareholding, usually at a price below the market price.

For CGT purposes rights issues are treated as follows:
- The rights shares are not treated as a separate holding of shares.
- The shares are treated as acquired on the same day as the original shares to which they relate.
- Therefore, the number of rights shares are included in the share pool, and the cost in the cost column in the same way as a normal purchase.

Sale of rights (nil paid)

Sales of rights (nil paid) = where shareholder does not take up rights issue and sells the 'right to buy' more shares.

The treatment of a 'sale of rights nil paid' for CGT purposes depends on the amount of sale proceeds (SP) received as follows:

If SP received are:	(i) > 5% of the value of the shares on which the rights are offered, **and** (ii) > £3,000.	(i) ≤ 5% of the value of the shares on which the rights are offered, **or** (ii) ≤ £3,000 if higher.
CGT treatment:	• deemed part disposal of original shares held. • normal part disposal computation required Where A = SP received B = MV of shares on which the rights are offered	• no chargeable disposal at the time of the sale of rights nil paid. • SP received are deducted from the cost of the original shares. • Taxpayer can elect for a part disposal if beneficial e.g. to utilise AEA

Exam focus

Exam kit questions on this area:

Section B question:
- Meg and Laurie

Takeovers and mergers

- Company (B) acquires shares in another company (A) by issuing shares to A's shareholders.
- 'Paper for paper'/'share for share' transaction = not a CGT disposal by A's shareholders.
  The new shares in B 'stand in shoes' of old A shares (i.e. take on the cost and acquisition date of A shares).
- Conditions:
  - clearance required from HMRC
  - B acquires > 25% of A's ordinary share capital (or a majority of the voting power of A)
  - the exchange is for bona fide commercial reasons and main purpose not the avoidance of tax.

With a share for share exchange, it is possible that:

- the old shares would qualify for BADR if it were treated as a disposal
- but the new company is not the shareholder's personal trading company and so the later disposal of its shares would not qualify for relief.

However, the individual shareholder can:

- elect for the event to be treated as a disposal for CGT purposes, in which case the gain is taxed at 0%, 10%, or 20% depending on the availability of the AEA, BADR, IR and level of taxable income.

If shares are sold for a mixture of cash and shares then a capital gain arises unless the cash element is small.

Takeovers

'Paper for paper' exchange
No CGT implications if satisfy conditions
- Clearance
- Acquire > 25%
- Bone fide reason

Mixture of 'paper' and cash

Cash element small
1. ≤ 5% of total value or
2. ≤ £3,000
→ No CGT implications at date of exchange

Cash element not small
1. > 5% of total value and
2. > £3,000
→ CGT implications at date of exchange re. cash received
→ Part disposal

Part disposal of cash element:

Cost of asset sold =

Original cost × $\frac{\text{Cash received}}{\text{Total consideration}}$

- Where consideration includes QCBs:
  - compute gain as if QCB was cash consideration
  - the frozen gain is charged when QCB sold.

Exam focus

Exam kit questions on this area:

Section B questions
- Pescara
- Liber

Capital gains tax – shares and securities

QCBs and government securities

- Disposal = exempt from CGT (i.e. no chargeable gain/no allowable loss).
- If received as consideration on a takeover and the share disposal is eligible for BADR, the taxpayer can either:
  - claim BADR at the takeover and the gain will be taxed at 10% at that time, or
  - not claim BADR at the takeover and the frozen gain will be taxed at the appropriate rate in force when it crystallises.

Definition

QCB: Normal commercial loan, expressed in sterling and not convertible into shares (e.g. company loan stock/loan notes).

Liquidations

- Shareholders are treated as having sold their shares for proceeds equal to the cash or other assets received from the liquidator.
- A chargeable gain or loss must be computed in the normal way.
- Consider pre-liquidation dividend payment.

Exam focus

Exam kit questions on this area:

Section A questions
- Joe and Fiona

Section B questions
- Acryl Ltd and Cresco Ltd

Losses on unquoted shares

- Capital losses are normally carried forward and offset against future capital gains.
- Can elect for a capital loss realised on the disposal of unquoted trading company shares to be treated as a trading loss.
- The capital loss can therefore be offset:
  - against income
  - of the tax year in which the loss arose, **and/or**
  - the preceding tax year.
- The shares must have been subscribed for, not purchased.

Capital gains tax – shares and securities

chapter

Capital gains tax – reliefs

In this chapter

- Overview of reliefs.
- Business asset disposal relief.
- Investors' relief.
- Private residence relief.
- PRR – periods of occupation.
- Rollover relief.
- Reinvestment in depreciating assets.
- Gift holdover relief.

Capital gains tax – reliefs

Exam focus

CGT reliefs are an important aspect of CGT in practice.

Given the examining team's approach to examining real life practical situations they are likely to continue to feature regularly in examination questions.

You may be required not just to calculate the reliefs but to state the conditions, when they apply and the tax implications.

Overview of reliefs

- After computing gains on disposals of individual assets consider the availability of reliefs.
- Some reliefs completely exempt a gain from CGT, or reduce the tax payable permanently, others only defer the gain to a later period.

Types of relief	
Permanent reliefs	**Deferral reliefs**
Business asset disposal relief	Rollover relief
Investors' relief	Gift holdover relief
Private residence relief	Incorporation relief (Chapter 16)
Letting relief	EIS reinvestment relief (Chapter 10)
SEIS reinvestment relief (Chapter 10)	

Business asset disposal relief (BADR)

- Only available to individuals.
- First £1 million of gains on 'qualifying business disposals' are taxed at 10%, regardless of the taxpayer's income.
- Any gains above the £1 million limit = taxed in full at 10% / 20%.
- Gains qualifying for BADR are set against any remaining basic rate band (BRB) before non-qualifying gains.
- The 10% CGT rate is calculated **after** the deduction of:
  - allowable losses, and
  - the AEA.
- Can choose to set losses and AEA against non-qualifying gains first to maximise relief.

  Exception:
  Any losses on assets forming part of the disposal of the business.
- Keep gains which qualify for BADR separate from those which do not qualify.
- For 2024/25 disposals, the relief must be claimed by 31 January 2027.
- £1 million = a lifetime limit (partly used up each time a claim is made).

Qualifying business disposals

The disposal of:

- the whole or part of an individual's trading business (i.e. sole trader or partner)
- assets of the individual's or partnership's trading business that has **now ceased**
- shares **provided**:
  - in the individual's 'personal trading company', **and**
  - the individual is an employee of the company (part time or full time).
- assets owned by the individual and used in a 'personal trading company' or trading partnership **provided**:
  - the individual also disposes of all or part of the partnership interest or shares in the personal trading company
  - as part of the individual's withdrawal of involvement in the partnership / company business.

An individual's 'personal trading company' is one where the individual:

- owns at least 5% of the ordinary shares
- which carry at least 5% of the voting rights.

When an individual disposes of goodwill to a close company (e.g. on incorporation) BADR is not available in respect of the goodwill, unless the individual:

- holds < 5% of the company's ordinary share capital or voting rights, or
- holds > 5% of the company's ordinary share capital or voting rights, but sells the whole shareholding to another company within 28 days.

Note that:
- "Part of a business"
  = a "substantial part" which is "capable of independent operation".
- Disposal of assets (i.e. not shares):
  Relief = not available on investment assets.
- No restriction to relief if company holds non-trading assets.
- No minimum working hours to satisfy employee condition.
- For approved EMI shares:
  no requirement to hold ≥ 5% shareholding.

Key Point

The isolated disposal of an **individual business asset** used for the purposes of a continuing trade does **not** qualify.

Qualifying ownership period
- 2 years prior to the disposal, or
- Where a qualifying business is not disposed of but simply ceases:
  - relief will be available on gains on assets in use in the business at the time it ceased
  - where the assets are disposed of within 3 years of the date of cessation.
- For approved EMI shares:
  - qualifying period runs from the date the option is granted (not when shares acquired).

Applying the relief

(1) Calculate the gains and losses on qualifying and non-qualifying assets separately.

(2) Net off losses relating to the qualifying business disposals against qualifying gains.

(3) Offset all other losses and the AEA against non-qualifying gains.

(4) If necessary deduct any remaining losses or AEA from the qualifying gains.

(5) Tax the gains as follows:
   – qualifying net chargeable gains at 10%
   – any non-qualifying net chargeable gains as normal at 10% or 20% (remember that qualifying gains utilise the BRB before non-qualifying gains).

Interaction of reliefs

- Other specific reliefs (if available) reduce chargeable gains before BADR is considered.
- If also eligible for BADR the remaining gain is taxable at 10%.

Exam focus

Exam kit questions on this area:

Section A questions
- Ziti
- Waverley and Set Ltd Group
- Sprint Ltd and Iron Ltd

Section B questions
- Ash
- Acryl Ltd and Cresco Ltd
- Mirtoon
- Max
- Sabin and Patan Ltd
- Yaqui

Investors' relief

BADR is only available on a share disposal if:

- the shares are in the individual's personal trading company (the individual holds 5% of the shares) and
- the individual is an officer or employee of the company.

Investors' relief extends the benefits of BADR to certain investors who would not meet the conditions for BADR.

IR applies to the disposal of:

- unlisted ordinary shares in a trading company (including AIM shares)
- subscribed for (i.e. newly issued shares) on/after 17 March 2016
- which have been held for a minimum period of 3 years starting on 6 April 2016
- by an individual who is not an employee of the company.

IR is subject to a separate lifetime limit of £10 million of qualifying gains.

Capital gains tax – reliefs

Private residence relief (PRR)

- Rules apply to house and garden (usually up to half a hectare)
- Owner occupied throughout
  - gain exempt
- Owner partly absent
  - PRR available

  Relief = Gain × $\frac{\text{Periods of occupation}}{\text{Period of ownership}}$

- If property partly let while owner occupied
  1. Calculate PRR relief
  2. Then give

     Letting relief:

     Lowest of:
     (i) £40,000
     (ii) PRR
     (iii) Gain re letting

PRR – periods of occupation

- Actual occupation.
- Deemed occupation.

Exam focus

You may be presented with an individual's personal circumstances and be required to assess the period of ownership of a property which will qualify for PRR.

You should provide brief explanatory notes for periods of deemed occupation.

Deemed occupation

Conditional	Unconditional

• Up to 3 years – any reason
• Any period – employed abroad
• Up to 4 years
  – working elsewhere in the UK (employed or self-employed)
  – working abroad if self-employed
• Must be actual occupation before and after
• Condition relaxed if reoccupation prevented by terms of employment
	• Last 9 months of ownership

Exam focus

Exam kit questions on this area:

Section B questions

- Mirtoon
- Demeter
- Yacon Ltd and Daikon
- Pinto
- Cada

Capital gains tax – reliefs

Rollover relief (ROR)

- Relief for the replacement of qualifying business assets (QBAs).
- The gain arising on the disposal of a QBA can be deferred if proceeds reinvested in replacement QBAs within a qualifying period.
- Available to:
  - companies, individual sole traders, partnerships.

Conditions

- Qualifying business assets
  - land and buildings
  - fixed plant and machinery
  - goodwill (unincorporated businesses only).
- Qualifying period
  - from 1 year before
  - to 3 years after the date of disposal
- Claim is made
  - within 4 years from the later of the end of the tax year of:
    - sale, and
    - replacement.
- For a 2024/25 disposal and replacement
  - by 5 April 2029.

Exam focus

ROR is the only relief available to companies. It is therefore more often tested in a corporate situation.

Effect of relief

Where all proceeds are reinvested:

- The full gain on the old asset is 'rolled over' against the capital gains cost of the new asset.
- No tax is payable when old asset sold.
- Gain deferred until the new asset sold.

Deferred gain is:

- deducted from the base cost of the replacement asset, and
- increases the gain on the subsequent disposal of the replacement asset.

Partial reinvestment of proceeds

Where all proceeds are **not** reinvested:

- The gain that can be rolled over (i.e. deferred) is restricted (i.e. not all of the gain can be deferred).
- A chargeable gain arises
  = **lower** of
  - the proceeds not reinvested
  - the chargeable gain.
- Taxable on the disposal of the original asset.
- The remaining gain is deferred.

Capital gains tax – reliefs

Procedure for calculating ROR

1. Calculate the gain on disposal of the trade asset.
2. Determine whether all sales proceeds have been reinvested in qualifying assets.

Proceeds fully reinvested	Proceeds not fully reinvested
No gain now	Gain now = Lower of: (i) total gain (B) (ii) proceeds not reinvested (C)
Gain rolled over A	Gain rolled over (D): D = B − C
CGT base cost of new asset: Cost X Gain rolled over (A) XX	CGT base cost of new asset: Cost X Gain rolled over (D) XX

Interaction with BADR

- BADR is only available if the entire business is being sold.

  There is no BADR on the disposal of an individual asset.

- If the entire business is sold and all the proceeds are reinvested into new qualifying assets:
  - consider ROR before BADR
  - the gains may be deferred
  - BADR only considered on subsequent disposal of replacement asset
  - based on conditions being satisfied that time.

- If partial reinvestment and some gain remains chargeable now:
  - will be taxed at 0%, 10%, or 20% depending on the availability of the AEA, BADR and level of taxable income
  - conditions for BADR considered now

Exam focus

Exam kit questions on this area:

Section A questions
- Dilip Group and Emma
- Hahn Ltd Group
- Hum Ltd Group
- Jeg Ltd Group

Section B questions
- Rabo Ltd
- Samphire Ltd and Kelp Ltd
- Fox Ltd

Reinvestment in depreciating assets

Definition

Depreciating asset (DA)
- life of ≤ 60 years

Common examples in exam:
- Fixed P&M
- Leasehold property of ≤ 60 years.

Method of relief

- Conditions and calculation of amount of relief = same as for ROR.
- Method of deferral = different.
- Gain not deducted from base cost of new asset.
- Gain is 'frozen' (i.e. deferred) and crystallises on the earliest of:
  - sale of DA
  - date DA ceases to be used in trade
  - 10 years from acquisition of DA.
- When deferred gain crystallises:
  - taxed at appropriate rate of CGT at that time (not at the time of deferral).
- Can defer a gain:
  - using a depreciating asset (for up to 10 years), and
  - later acquire a non-depreciating asset, and
  - claim to rollover the deferred gain instead (i.e. defer indefinitely until the replacement non-depreciating asset is sold)
  - provided the deferred gain has not previously become chargeable.

Exam focus

Exam kit questions on this area:

Section A questions

- Sprint Ltd and Iron Ltd

Section B questions

- Hyssop Ltd
- Fox Ltd
- Yaqui

Gift holdover relief (Gift relief – GR)

The gain arising on a gift is computed by using the market value of the asset.

GR must then be considered.

Recipient
Individual, trustee or company R in UK at time of gift

Applies to
Gifts and Sales at undervalue by individuals and trustees (not companies)

Effect
Deemed consideration = MV
Gain deferred against base cost to donee

Individual donor

Qualifying assets
(1) Assets used in trade of donor or by donor's personal trading company (i.e. owns ≥ 5% voting rights)
(2) Shares in unquoted trading company
(3) Shares in donor's personal trading company
(4) Any asset where there is an immediate charge to IHT (e.g. gift into trust)
(5) Agricultural property eligible for APR

Asset not wholly used for business
Only gain related to trade use is deferred.
For shares (if own ≥ 5% voting rights) proportion of gain qualifying for relief is:

$$\frac{\text{MV Chargeable business assets}}{\text{MV Chargeable assets}}$$

Capital gains tax – reliefs

Key Point

Restriction of (CBA/CA) only applies where donor holds ≥ 5% of shares.

If donor holds < 5% of shares:
- unquoted = no restrictions to GR
- quoted = no GR

Sale at undervaluation

Where the asset is sold, but for less than MV the 'actual consideration' received is ignored

- The gain is still calculated using MV.

If the actual consideration > transferor's cost
- the excess is immediately chargeable
- the remaining gain can be deferred.

The chargeable gain arising now will be:
- taxed on the donor at either 0%, 10%, or 20%
- depending on the availability of the AEA BADR/IR or the level of taxable income.

If the actual consideration ≤ donor's cost:
- full gift holdover relief available
- all chargeable gain deferred.

The deferred gain is taxed on the donee later at the appropriate rate when the asset is disposed of.

Emigration of donee

If within 6 yrs of gift the donee emigrates:

- the deferred gain crystallises on the donee
- on the day before emigration.

Effect of relief

Regardless of how the gain is calculated, the deferred gain is:

- deducted from the base cost of the donee, and
- deferred until the subsequent disposal of the asset by the donee.

When the gain crystallises:

- taxed at appropriate rate of CGT at that time (not at the time of deferral).

Election

For a gift in 2024/25, a joint election is required:

- signed by both the donor and donee
- by 5 April 2029.

If gift into a trust:

- only needs to be signed by the settlor.

Exam focus

Exam kit questions on this area:

Section A questions

- Ziti
- Jake
- Mita and Snowdon

Section B questions

- Surfe
- Max
- Anya

Capital gains tax – reliefs

Interaction with BADR

- If BADR is applicable:
  - the donor may choose not to claim gift holdover relief in order to crystallise a gain and claim BADR now instead.
- This is advantageous if the donee will not qualify for the relief on the subsequent disposal. For example, if the donee would not satisfy the employment condition and/or 2 year ownership rule.

- If the individual disposes of shares in a personal trading company:
  - gift holdover relief is available:
    - subject to the (CBA / CA) restriction above
    - regardless of whether the individual works for the company
  - If a gain remains after gift holdover relief (due to the CBA/CA restriction) then BADR will also be available provided:
    - the individual works for the company, and
    - it has been the individual's personal trading company
    - for the 2 years prior to the disposal.

chapter

7

Stamp taxes

In this chapter

- Stamp duty and stamp duty land tax.

Stamp taxes

Exam focus

Stamp taxes may feature as part of a question, however a question will not be set exclusively on stamp taxes.

Stamp duty and stamp duty land tax

- Paid by purchaser.

Stamp Duty (SD) / Stamp Duty Reserve Tax (SDRT)	Stamp Duty Land Tax (SDLT)
Payable on	
• transfer shares/securities	• transactions in UK property
Rate	
• 0.5% of consideration	• up to 5% of commercial property depending on amount of consideration (note)
• SD only:	
– min £5	• rates given in tax rates and allowances
– no charge if consideration ≤ £1,000	

Note: Only commerical property will be tested in the examination.

Specific exemptions	
Stamp Duty (SD) / Stamp Duty Reserve Tax (SDRT)	**Stamp Duty Land Tax (SDLT)**

• Exempt securities
  – government stock
  – most company loan stock (unless convertible)
  – unit trusts
  – AIM shares.	

General exemptions	

• Gifts
• Transfers of assets between 75% group companies
  – not available if arrangements in force for purchasing company to leave group
  – SDLT exemption relief withdrawn if transferee company leaves group within 3 years of transfer, still owning the land.	

Stamp taxes

Exam focus

Exam Kit questions on this area:

Section A questions

- Grand Ltd Group
- Heyer Ltd Group
- Dilip Group and Emma
- Gail and Brad
- Hum Ltd Group

chapter 8

Inheritance tax

In this chapter

- Charge to inheritance tax.
- Lifetime gifts.
- IHT computations.
- Due dates of payment.
- Valuation.
- Exemptions and reliefs.
- Death estate pro forma.
- Payment by instalments.
- Deed of variation.
- Married couples and civil partners.
- IHT and CGT on sales/gifts.
- Skipping a generation.

Inheritance tax

Exam focus

Inheritance tax regularly features in the ATX exam, often as part of a question involving other taxes too – particularly capital gains tax.

Charge to inheritance tax (IHT)

- Occasions of charge:
  - Lifetime gifts.
  - Death estate.
- Charged on:
  - a chargeable transfer (later)
  - of chargeable property
  - by a chargeable person.
- Chargeable property:
  - all capital assets / wealth
  - no exempt assets for IHT.
- Chargeable person:
  - individuals.
- Gratuitous intent:
  - transfer must be a gift
  - intention to give asset away
  - not a poor business deal.

Lifetime gifts

- Two types:
  - Potentially Exempt Transfers (PETs)
  - Chargeable Lifetime Transfers (CLTs)

	PETs	CLTs	
Definition	Gift by individual to: • another individual • a disabled trust • certain old trusts (not examinable)	Gift which is not: • Exempt, or • a PET Main examples = gifts to trusts: • (except charitable trusts or those treated as PETs)	
Chargeable	Only if donor dies within 7 years of gift	At date of gift	Additional IHT if donor dies within 7 years of gift
Tax rates	Death rates	Lifetime rates	Death rates
Tax paid by	Donee	Donee, or Donor (gross up gift for tax paid)	Donee

IHT computations

Exam focus

An IHT charge can arise in 3 different situations. The computation in each situation is different and must be studied carefully.

1. Lifetime transfers – IHT on CLTs
2. Death – additional IHT on PETs and CLTs
3. Death estate

In each situation:

- Compute the chargeable transfer.
- Compute the taxable amount.
- Compute the tax.

The chargeable transfer

The first stage of the computation for each situation is always the same; calculate the chargeable transfer:

	£	
Transfer of value:		
Value before	X	– Diminution in value principle
Value after	(X)	– Related property
	X	
Deduct:		
(1) Reliefs	(X)	– APR – BPR
(2) Exemptions	(X)	– (later in chapter)
Chargeable transfer	A	

Order of using reliefs and exemptions – later in chapter.

Calculating the taxable amount

Calculating the taxable amount is also the same for each situation. However, the calculation of the available nil rate bands (NRBs) differs.

	£
Chargeable transfer	A
Less:	
Available NRBs	(X)
Taxable amount	X

Nil rate bands

- For lifetime gifts – lifetime tax:
  - Use NRB in tax year of gift.
- For lifetime gifts – death tax:
  - Use NRB in tax year of death.
- For death estate:
  - Use NRB in tax year of death
  - Calculate the available residence nil rate band (RNRB).
- The NRBs will be provided in the tax rates and allowances.

Residence nil rate band (RNRB)

- For lifetime gifts – not available.
- For death estate – available if residential property left to direct descendants (children/grandchildren).
- Deceased must have lived in the property.
- Available RNRB will be lower of:
  - £175,000
  - net value of residential property.

Tapered withdrawal of RNRB

- If net value of estate (before APR, BPR and exemptions) > £2 million
  - reduce RNRB by £1 for every £2 of excess.

Inheritance tax

Exam focus

Exam kit questions in this area:

Section A questions
- Ziti
- Pippin
- Jake
- Gail and Brad
- Olma and Hogan

Section B questions
- Tula
- Pescara
- Eric
- Liber
- Luis

Calculating the tax

1 – Lifetime tax on CLT

	£	£
Chargeable transfer (A)		222,000
Less:		
NRB at gift (say)	312,000	
Less: CLTs in 7 years prior to gift (say)	(170,000)	
NRB available		(142,000)
Taxable amount		80,000
IHT payable:		
(i) at 20% if donee pays tax		16,000
(ii) at 25% if donor pays tax		20,000

If donor pays tax:
Add IHT to value of chargeable transfer (A) to calculate gross chargeable amount (B)
i.e. (£222,000 + £20,000) = £242,000

Key Point

Note that the donor is primarily responsible for the lifetime tax due.

2 – Additional tax on lifetime transfers as a result of donor's death

Perform the following calculation for:
- each gift (CLTs and PETs) in the 7 years prior to death
- in chronological order

Gift 1 – CLT or PET

	£	£
Gross chargeable transfer (A or B)		365,000
Less:		
NRB at death	325,000	
Less: CLTs and chargeable PETs in 7 years prior to gift (1) (say)	(140,000)	
NRB available		(185,000)
Taxable amount		180,000

Inheritance tax

	£
IHT payable at 40%	72,000
Less: Taper relief (40%)(say)	(28,800)
Chargeable (60%)	43,200
Less: Lifetime tax paid (say)	(10,000)
IHT payable	33,200

Then perform the same calculation for Gift 2 etc.

Notes:

(a) Order of using reliefs and exemptions:

1. Exempt gifts, small, spouse, charity
2. APR
3. BPR
4. Fall in value
5. ME
6. AE current year, then b/f
7. Taper relief

(b) Taper relief

Years before death	% reduction
Over 3 but less than 4 years	20%
Over 4 but less than 5 years	40%
Over 5 but less than 6 years	60%
Over 6 but less than 7 years	80%

(c) Lifetime tax deduction:

– cannot create a repayment of IHT.

3 – IHT on death estate

Death estate computation:

	£	£
Value of estate (includes home)		1,025,000
Less:		
RNRB (max)	175,000	
NRB at death	325,000	
Less: CLTs and chargeable PETs in 7 years prior to death (say)	(255,000)	
NRB available		(245,000)
Taxable amount		780,000
IHT payable at 40%		312,000
Less: Quick succession relief		(X)
Double taxation relief		(X)
IHT payable		X

Due dates of payment

1 Lifetime IHT

Gift:	Due date:
6 April – 30 Sept	30 April in next year
1 Oct – 5 April	6 months after end of month of gift

2 Additional IHT on lifetime gifts due to death

Due date – 6 months from end of month of death.

Note: always paid by donee.

3 IHT on death estate

Due date – 6 months from end of month of death.

However, tax is required to be paid with delivery of accounts to HMRC, which may be earlier than due date.

Inheritance tax

Valuation

Exam focus

An exam question, particularly one involving the death estate, will also require you to value the assets being transferred.

1 Gifts

- IHT uses the 'diminution in value' principle to calculate the 'transfer of value' (i.e. value by which the donor's estate has been reduced).

	£
Value of estate before transfer	X
Less: Value of estate after transfer	(X)
Transfer of value	X

- In most cases = value of asset gifted
- In some cases the diminution in value > value of asset gifted
  - e.g. gift of unquoted shares.

Key Point

It is important to appreciate the difference here between CGT and IHT.

For CGT purposes the consideration used for a gift = valued at the market value of the asset gifted.

2 Related property

- Special rules where same type of property owned by:
  - Spouse/civil partner, or
  - Exempt body (e.g. charity) as a result of an exempt transfer to them by the donor or the donor's spouse/civil partner.
- Applies when valuing a gift or an asset in an individual's estate.

- Value of asset – 2 situations:

    (i) **All assets except unquoted shares**

    $$\frac{\text{Value of individual's share}}{\text{Value of individual's share + Related party share}} \times \text{Value of combined assets}$$

    (ii) **Unquoted shares**

    Use the same formula, but the 'number' of shares is used in the fraction, not the value.

Exam focus

The related property rules are often relevant in exam questions involving unquoted shares.

3 Other assets

General rule	Open Market Value
Quoted shares and securities	Lower of: 1/4 up rule and the average of the highest and lowest marked bargains.
Unquoted shares	No readily available market price – will vary depending on % holding. Value agreed with HMRC. In examination – value will normally be given.
Unit trusts	Lower bid price
UK freehold property	Jointly owned property: • Valuation ÷ number of joint owners. • Joint tenants – share passes automatically (not via will) to joint tenant. • Tenants in common – share inherited according to will. Value reduced by mortgage.
Life assurance	On own life = actual proceeds received • For benefit of named beneficiary under a declaration of trust – excluded from estate.

Exemptions and reliefs

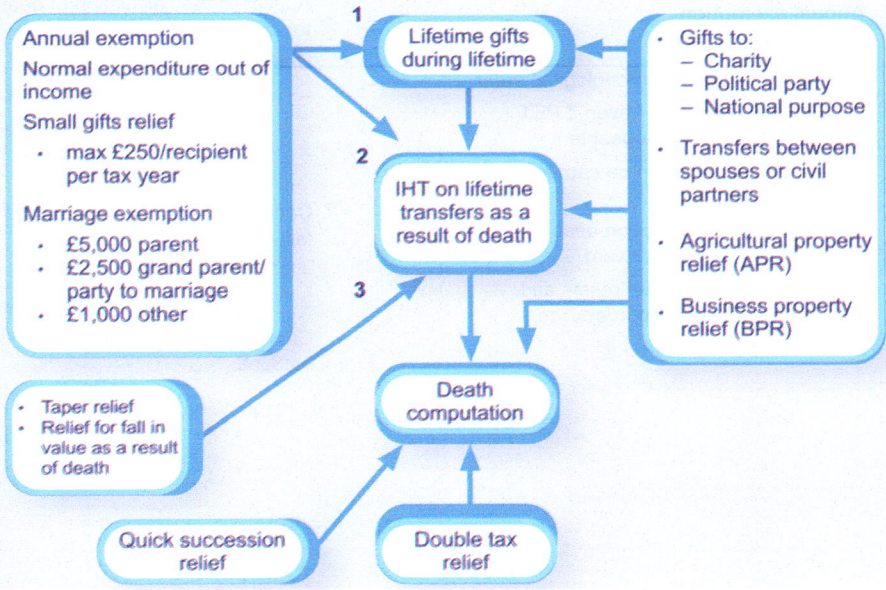

Inheritance tax

Key exemptions and reliefs

1 Annual exemption

- £3,000 per annum
- Applied to gifts in chronological order
- Used against PET – even if PET never becomes chargeable
- Unused amount can be carried forward one year
- Current year exemption used in priority to brought forward
- Applied after all other reliefs and exemptions have been applied.

2 Fall in value relief

- Applies in the calculation of death tax on PETs and CLTs.
- Donee must:
  - still own the asset at date of donor's death, or
  - have sold it in arm's length transaction.
- Deduct from chargeable amount the fall in value:
  - from: date of gift
  - to: date of death or earlier sale.
- Carry forward original chargeable amount.

Exam focus

Exemptions and reliefs will always feature in an IHT computation – it is important that you can identify when they are available and how they are applied.

Exam focus

Exam kit questions with exemptions and reliefs:

Section A questions
- Ziti

Section B questions
- Pescara
- Max
- Cada
- Liber

3 Business property relief (BPR)

Two key conditions:
- Transfer of relevant business property (RBP).
- Minimum period of ownership.

Exam focus

This relief is extremely important and can be expected to feature in almost every examination.

- Applies to lifetime transfers and on death.
- Applies to relevant business property.

Inheritance tax

Relevant business property (RBP)

Property	Conditions	Relief
Quoted shares and securities	• Out of a controlling interest • Must be trading company	50%
Unquoted shares and securities	• Including AIM • Must be trading company • Only available on securities if have control based on shares	100%
Assets	• Land and buildings, P&M: – Used by company controlled by donor, or – Used by a partnership in which donor is a partner	50%

Property	Conditions	Relief
Sole trader	• Unincorporated business or share in partnership • Must be the whole business not individual assets	100%

- Available on UK and overseas RBP.
- Not available on excepted assets (e.g. investments).
- Where company owns investments BPR is given on:

$$\text{Value of shares} \times \frac{\text{Company's business property}}{\text{Company's total assets (before liabilities)}}$$

Length of ownership

- Property must have been owned for ≥ 2 years (unless replacement property).
- Where business property was inherited and was eligible for BPR at that time:
  - there is no minimum ownership period for BPR on the second death (successive transfers rule).
- Where business property is transferred from a spouse/civil partner:
  - the combined length of ownership by the couple is considered.

Death tax on lifetime gifts

- Where additional IHT due on gift as a result of donor's death:
  - BPR only available where business property is still owned by the donee at the date of the donor's death.

Tax planning

- No IHT payable on assets which qualify for 100% BPR.
- No IHT saving from making lifetime gifts of assets which qualify for 100% BPR, better to gift on death.

Exam focus

Exam kit questions on this area:

Section A questions

- Ziti
- Jake
- Gail and Brad
- Plad Ltd and Quil Ltd

Section B questions

- Eric
- Tula
- Anya

4 Agricultural Property Relief (APR)

- Applies to lifetime transfers and on death.
- Applies to the **agricultural value** of relevant agricultural property.
- Agricultural property = farmland, pastures and farm buildings.
- Only available on agricultural property situated in UK or EEA.
- Rate of relief = 100%.

Exam focus

Exam kit questions on this area:

Section B questions

- Eric
- Joan Ark

Length of ownership

- Property must have been owned for:

Agricultural property farmed by:	Ownership
The owner	Two years
A tenant	Seven years

- Successive transfers and spouse/civil partner transfer rules as per BPR.

Death tax on lifetime gifts

- Retention rules as per BPR.

Tax planning

- No IHT saving from making lifetime gifts which qualify for APR, better to gift on death.

Death estate pro forma

	Notes	£	£
Freehold property		x	
Less: Mortgage	(a)	(x)	
			x
Foreign property		x	
Less: Expenses	(b)	(x)	
			x
			x
All other assets owned by deceased			x
Debts due to deceased			x
Accrued income			x
			x
Less: Outstanding debts	(c)		(x)
			x
Less: Exempt legacies	(d)		(x)
			x
Gift with reservation (GWR)	(e)		x
Chargeable estate			x

IHT payable computation

	£	£
Chargeable estate		x
RNRB available		(x)
NRB at death	325,000	
Less: GCT's in previous 7 years	(x)	
NRB available		(x)
Taxable estate		x
IHT on taxable estate (40% or 36%)		x
Less: Quick succession relief		(x)
		A

$$\text{Average estate rate (AER)} = \frac{A}{\text{Chargeable estate}} \times 100$$

Less: Double tax relief		(x)
Inheritance tax payable		B

Due date:

Earlier of
- 6 months after the end of the month of death, or
- On delivery of the estate accounts
  (unless paid by instalments – covered later)

Inheritance tax

Allocation of UK IHT payable:

- IHT payable on estate = apportioned at AER (after QSR)
- Tax paid by:

GWR	Recipient of gift
Remainder	
– overseas asset	Recipient of legacy (tax bearing gift)
– UK asset	Residuary legatee (tax-free gift)

Key Point

All assets are chargeable (i.e. no exempt assets for IHT at ATX).

Assets that are exempt from CGT (e.g. cars, gilts, ISAs, PRR etc) are not exempt from IHT.

Notes

(a) Repayment and interest-only mortgages and accrued interest.

(b) Expenses restricted to maximum 5% of foreign property value.

(c) Outstanding debts payable by the deceased (e.g. outstanding bills and other taxes due: IT, CGT, VAT).

(d) Exempt legacies = legacies to spouse, civil partner, charity, political party.

(e) Gifts with reservation = lifetime gift where donor retains a benefit (e.g. gift of legal title to house but donor still lives in it).
   - bring into estate computation as if gift never made
   - can be avoided if donor pays market rate rent to donee.

Exam focus

Exam kit questions with a gift with reservation:

Section A questions
- Drench, Paprikash, Hail Ltd and Rain Ltd

Section B questions
- Pescara
- Pedro
- Yacon Ltd and Daikon
- Mirtoon

Substantial legacies to charity

- Reduced rate of 36% applies to estates where:
  - total charitable legacies on death $\geq$ 10% x (baseline amount).
- Baseline amount
  = Taxable estate
  plus charitable legacies plus residence nil rate band.
- Can use a deed of variation to increase a charitable legacy to benefit from the 36% rate.

Quick Succession Relief (QSR)

- Look for gifts to the deceased in the five years before death
- Tax credit relief
- QSR = (IHT on first gift) x appropriate %
- IHT on first death = (estate rate on first death) x value of the legacy
- Percentages:

Years between first transfer and date of death		Appropriate % to use in formula
More Than	Not more than	
0	1	100%
1	2	80%
2	3	60%
3	4	40%
4	5	20%

- Given before DTR

Double Tax Relief (DTR)

- Lower of
    (i) overseas tax suffered
    (ii) AER x (overseas property value brought into estate)

Payment by instalments

- Elect to pay in ten equal annual instalments.
- Only the following assets qualify:
  - land and buildings
  - unincorporated businesses
  - shares or securities where the donor has a controlling interest
  - some unquoted shares and securities (detail not examinable).
- Available on
  - death estate
  - PETs and CLTs which become chargeable on death, and
  - CLTs where the donee pays the tax.
- If asset sold in instalment period outstanding balance must be paid immediately.

Exam focus

Examination questions on IHT will usually involve an element of planning, including advising on how a transfer of assets could be organised more effectively for IHT purposes (Chapter 15).

Inheritance tax

Deed of variation

- To change the distribution of assets under will or intestacy.
- Conditions:
  - all beneficiaries must agree
  - must be in writing
  - must contain clause that it is to be effective for IHT purposes
  - made within 2 years of death.
- Situations when useful:
  - to skip a generation where children wealthy in own right
  - to divert family home to direct descendants (children or grandchildren) to use RNRB
  - to increase a charitable donation to benefit from the reduced 36% rate on death estate.

Married couples and civil partners

Exempt transfers

- Inter-spouse / civil partner transfers = exempt
  - unlimited in amount
- Exception = if recipient spouse / civil partner is non-UK domiciled
  - maximum exemption = current NRB

Election to be treated as UK domiciled

- Non-UK domiciled spouse / civil partner
  - can elect to be treated as UK domiciled
  - irrevocable election
  - by individual in lifetime, or by executors within 2 years of death of individual.
- Advantage = unlimited inter-spouse / civil partner exemption.
- Disadvantage = subject to IHT on overseas assets.

Transfer of unused nil rate bands

- If the NRB/RNRB has not been utilised at the time of a person's death, the proportion of the unused NRB/RNRB can be transferred to the surviving spouse or civil partner.
- Surviving spouse or civil partner will have the benefit of:
  - own NRB/RNRB, and
  - any unused percentage of spouse's or civil partner's NRB/RNRB.
- The unused percentage is applied to the NRB/RNRB at the time of the surviving spouse's or civil partner's death
  - **not** at the date of first death.
- The executors of the surviving spouse or civil partner must claim the transferred NRB/RNRB by the submission of the IHT return by the later of :
  - 2 years of the second death, or
  - 3 months of the executors starting to act.
- As a result, each spouse or civil partner can leave the whole of estate to the surviving spouse or civil partner with no adverse IHT consequences.

Inheritance tax

Exam focus

Exam kit questions on this area:

Section B questions

- Pescara

Tax planning

Advice for couples:

- Where the couple own assets that qual. for BPR and/or APR these assets shoul **not** be left to the other spouse or civil partner.

    This is because the legacy would be covered by the inter-spouse exemption and the benefit of BPR and APR is lost.

- BPR and APR assets should be left to non-exempt beneficiaries and other assets left to the spouse or civil partner.

    As a result, the benefit of both the relief and inter-spouse exemption will be available to reduce the value of the chargeable estate.

IHT and CGT on sales/gifts

Examination questions dealing with capital transactions may require consideration of both the IHT and CGT implications of transactions.

	CGT	IHT
Sale	Gain/loss in normal way	No IHT – no diminution in estate
Gift during lifetime	As for sale Gain/loss in normal way	CLT – tax now PET – tax if die within 7 years
Gift on death	No CGT	Asset part of death estate
Possible reliefs – Business assets	BADR Investors' relief Gift holdover relief Rollover relief EIS/SEIS reinvestment relief	APR/BPR **Note:** On a PET or CLT – reliefs only available if asset still owned by donee at date of donor's death
– Non-business	PRR Gift holdover relief if CLT for IHT purposes EIS/SEIS reinvestment relief	None

Inheritance tax

Advantage of lifetime gifts	Disadvantages of lifetime gifts

- Reduces IHT payable on death as assets gifted during lifetime are removed from the chargeable estate.
 	
  Note: no reduction in the value of the chargeable estate if the assets gifted get BPR or APR at 100%.
 	
- IHT on lifetime gifts likely to be less than IHT in death estate because:
  – IHT = Nil (for a PET) if the donor lives for > 7 years, and 20% (for CLT)
  – the value is frozen at the date of the gift, therefore by gifting an appreciating asset during lifetime, the IHT is based on a lower amount, and fall in value relief is available if fallen in value
  – the value subject to IHT is less as lifetime exemptions (such as AE, ME, small gift relief) available
  – taper relief available if the donor lives for > 3 years.
	- Loss of income and use of the capital if assets given away.
	- CGT may be payable if the assets gifted during lifetime are chargeable assets for CGT, whereas no CGT if gifted on death.
	- APR or BPR on lifetime gift withdrawn if donee does not retain asset at donor death. Therefore better to secure BPR/APR by retaining asset in donor's estate.
	- No RNRB available if residential property gifted in lifetime.

Exam focus

Exam kit questions on this area:

Section B questions
- Cada
- Liber

Skipping a generation
- Gifting to grandchildren rather then children avoids a further IHT charge when the children die.
- Such planning requires children to be independently wealthy, such that they have no need for the inheritance.

Inheritance tax

chapter 9

Trusts

In this chapter

- Overview of trusts.
- Types of trust.
- Financial planning benefits of trusts.
- Income tax.
- Capital taxes and trusts.

Trusts

Overview of trusts

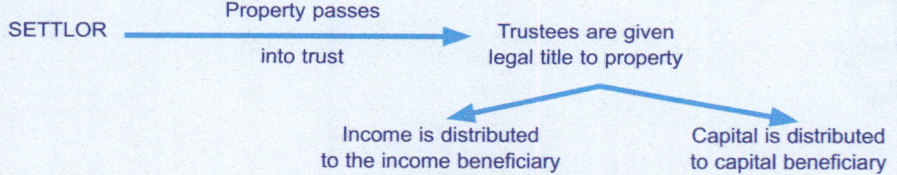

- Trust (also known as a settlement) = Treated as separate taxable person.
- Must have > one trustee.
- Trustees = act in representative capacity in best interests of beneficiaries.
- Trust deed = details trustee's powers and duties.

Exam focus

In recognition of the complexity of trusts, the examining team has confirmed that the knowledge required in relation to trusts is limited to the information summarised in this chapter.

Types of trust

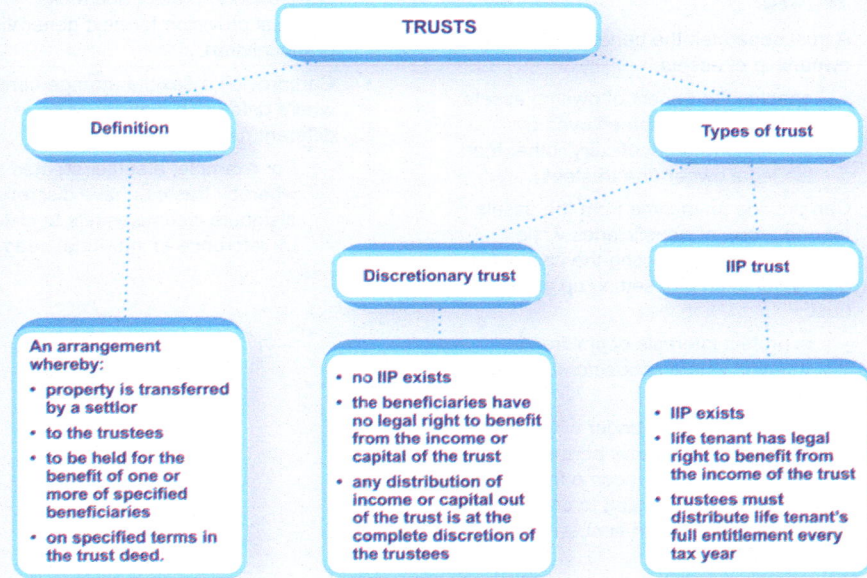

Financial planning benefits of trusts

- A trust separates the beneficial and legal ownership of assets:
  - enables the benefit of owning assets (e.g. income), to be enjoyed by someone (the beneficiary) other than the legal owner (the trustees).
- Can provide an income from the assets for one group of beneficiaries while preserving and protecting the capital for others, for example, setting up an IIP trust:
  - to protect interests of children in situation where spouse/civil partner remarries
  - to transfer assets under will to IIP trust with spouse/civil partner (life tenant) entitled to income for life and capital assets passing to children (remaindermen) on spouse/civil partner's death.
- Can provide a means for an older generation to protect and make financial provision for next generation or grandchildren.
- Can provide a flexible arrangement where different beneficiaries have different needs.
  - For example, a settlor creates a DT whereby trustees have discretion to distribute income/assets to children by reference to individual need.

Income tax

- Trustees = separate taxable person.
- Income tax paid by trustees under self-assessment on income generated by trust and by beneficiaries on income received.

Type	Trustees	Beneficiaries
IIP	Depends on type of income: • dividends 8.75% • savings 20% • non-savings 20%	• Life tenant entitled to trust income. • Taxed in year of entitlement (not year of receipt). • Income maintains nature in beneficiaries' hands (i.e. savings income and other income grossed up by 100/80 with a 20% tax credit, dividend income grossed up by 100/91.25 with 8.75% tax credit).
DT	Different rates – calculation not examinable	• Taxed on income actually received in tax year. • Always grossed up at 100/55 with 45% tax credit. • Taxed as non-savings income.

Trusts

Capital taxes and trusts

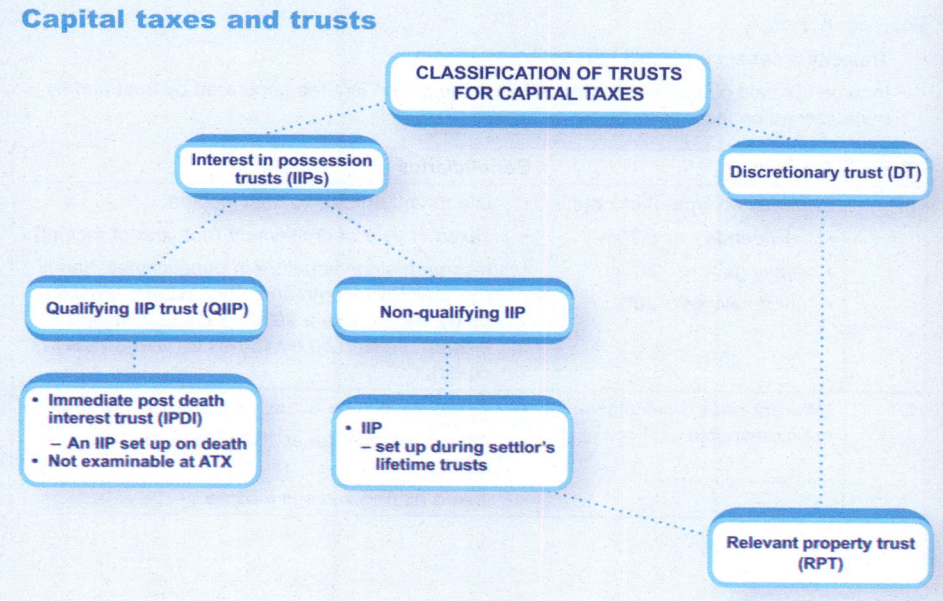

Inheritance tax

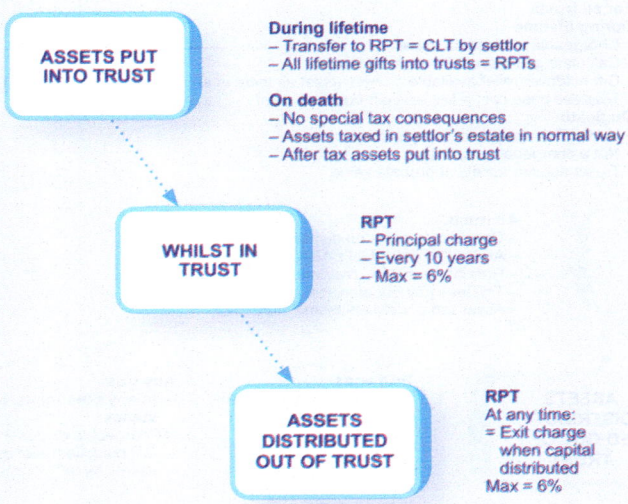

Trusts

Capital Gains Tax

ASSETS PUT INTO TRUST

For all trusts
During lifetime
– Chargeable disposal of asset
– Calculate gain using MV as consideration
– Gift holdover relief available on ANY asset as there is an immediate charge to IHT
– Trustees base cost = MV less gift holdover relief

On death
– No CGT consequences on death
– Not a chargeable disposal
– Trusts acquire assets at probate value

WHILST IN TRUST

All trusts
– Chargeable gains on disposals by trustees
– AEA = half individual's AEA (£1,500 in 2024/25)
– Rate of tax = 20% (residential property 24%)
– Trustees pay out of trust fund
– Assessed under self-assessment rules

ASSETS DISTRIBUTED OUT OF TRUST

IPDI ends
– interest ends on death of life tenant
= No CGT
= Tax free uplift to MV
Remainderman receives assets at MV on life tenant's death

Any trust
– in any other circumstances
= Chargeable disposal
– Gift holdover relief on ANY assets as IHT charge

Tax planning opportunities

- Gifting assets into a trust during lifetime
  - means that assets not in settlor's estate on death.
- Assets which appreciate in value can be transferred into the trust
  - will increase in value outside of both the settlor's and the beneficiaries estates.
- Exit charges and principal charges = max 6%
  - may not be significant in the context of the financial planning requirements.
- Trustees of a DT can choose to give income to non-tax paying beneficiaries
  - repayment of income tax paid by the trustees can be claimed.

Exam focus

Exam kit questions on this area:

Section B questions

- Alex

Trusts

chapter 10

Ethics, personal financial management and self-assessment

In this chapter

- Professional Code of Ethics.
- Monitoring of serious tax offenders.
- Personal financial management.
- Key investment products.
- Tax efficient investment schemes.
- EIS reinvestment relief
- SEIS reinvestment relief
- Sources of finance.
- Self-assessment.

Ethics, personal financial management and self-assessment

Exam focus

This chapter covers the very important topics of ethics, professional issues, personal financial management and self-assessment.

The examining team has stated that there will always be 5 marks in section A of each examination allocated to the topic of ethics and professional issues.

Questions will require you to provide practical advice based on a particular set of facts.

You need a good knowledge of the professional code of ethics and the investment products available.

You must be able to give suitable advice based on the facts of a particular scenario.

Professional Code of Ethics

Principles
- **O**bjectivity.
- **P**rofessional behavour.
- **P**rofessional competence.
- **I**ntegrity.
- **C**onfidentiality.

Key Point

Remember: OPPIC.

Exam focus

Exam kit questions on this area:

Section A questions
- Drench, Paprikash, Hail Ltd and Rain Ltd
- Jonny
- Olma and Hogan

New clients

Before taking on a new client – a member of ACCA must assess:

- risk to the integrity of the practice on accepting work
- whether firm has adequate skills and competence
- risk of money laundering.

Information to be obtained:

- For a company
  - proof of incorporation, primary business address and registered office
  - structure, directors and shareholders of the company
  - identities of persons instructing the firm on behalf of the company and persons authorised to do so.
- For an individual
  - proof of identity and residential address
  - details of nature and structure of any unincorporated business interests and persons authorised to act on behalf of the business (e.g. partners in a partnership).

On accepting work – a member of ACCA:

- must ask permission from the client to contact old advisers to request information
- if client refuses, should consider not acting for them
- if not, issue a letter of engagement setting out terms and conditions.

Exam focus

Exam kit questions on this area:

Section A questions

- Jeg Ltd Group
- Joe and Fiona
- Jake

Conflicts of interest

- Examples:
  - asked to act for another party in a transaction with an existing client
  - acting for both parties in a divorce
  - acting for the employer and their employees
  - where the adviser may benefit from the transaction.
- A member of ACCA may act for both parties if safeguards put in place:
  - the potential conflict should be pointed out to all relevant parties
  - consent should be obtained to act for them
  - the firm must have clear guidelines in relation to confidentiality, and
  - should consider the need to use separate teams for each client.
- Alternatively, consider acting for just one party, or not acting for either party.

Exam focus

Exam kit questions on this area:

Section A questions

- Mita and Snowdon
- Olma and Hogan

Dealing with HMRC

- Information provided must be accurate and complete.
- Must not assist a client to plan or commit an offence.
- If become aware of a tax irregularity:
  - discuss with client
  - ensure proper disclosure to HMRC.
- Client error:
  - decide whether genuine or deliberate/fraudulent act
  - explain to client the need to notify HMRC
  - prompt/adequate disclosure taken into account when deciding penalties
  - if client refuses:
    - must explain potential consequences in writing
    - if material, consider whether to continue to act for client
  - if client still refuses
    - should cease to act and write to HMRC stating that the firm no longer acts for the client but not stating the reason why.

Exam focus

Exam kit questions on this area:

Section A questions

- Ziti
- Gail and Brad
- Hahn Ltd Group
- Heyer Ltd Group and Dee
- Plad Ltd and Quil Ltd
- Hum Ltd Group

Money laundering regulations

Definition

Money laundering = benefiting from or concealing the proceeds of crime
- includes the proceeds of tax evasion.

A member of ACCA must appoint a Money laundering reporting officer (MLRO):
- MLRO decides whether to report a transaction to the National Crime Agency (NCA)
- if a report is made, client should not be informed as this is an offence (known as 'tipping off').

Employees

If a member is an employee and becomes aware of irregularities in his/her/their firm's dealings with HMRC:
- raise concerns with the appropriate person
- if appropriate action not taken
  - seek advice from ACCA
- in addition, consider:
  - need to report to MLRO
  - resigning from employment
  - need to disclose under the Public Interest Disclosure Act.

Tax evasion versus tax avoidance

- Tax evasion
  - unlawful
  - e.g. suppressing information or submitting false information
  - client = subject to criminal prosecution / fines / imprisonment
  - adviser = subject to sanctions of criminal law.
- Tax avoidance
  - use of the taxation system to legitimately reduce tax
  - e.g. advice to reduce tax liability
  - also used to describe tax schemes devised to utilise loopholes in the tax legislation.
- Specific schemes have been targeted with anti-avoidance legislation.

- HMRC have also introduced:
  - Disclosure obligations re specific tax avoidance schemes.
  - A general anti-abuse rule (GAAR) to counter artificial and abusive schemes to avoid tax.

    This targets arrangements which cannot be regarded as a reasonable course of action.
- Serial tax avoidance
  - Those who persistently engage in tax avoidance schemes defeated by HMRC = subject to a regime of increasing penalties and may have their details published by HMRC.

Exam focus

Exam kit questions on this area:

Section A questions

- Grand Ltd Group

Monitoring of serious tax offenders

Those who:

- incur a penalty for deliberate evasion
- in respect of tax of £5,000 or more

will be required to submit returns:

- for up to the following 5 years
- showing more detailed business accounts information, and
- detailing the nature and value of any balancing adjustments within the accounts.

Dishonest conduct of tax agents

- Incurs a civil penalty of up to £50,000.
- In cases where full disclosure was not made, HMRC may:
  - publish details of the penalised tax agent
  - access the working papers of a dishonest agent with agreement of the Tax tribunal.

Publication of names of tax offenders

- HMRC have the power to publish:
  - the names and details
  - of individuals and companies
  - who are penalised for deliberate defaults leading to a loss of tax of > £25,000.
- Names will not be published of:
  - those who make a full unprompted disclosure, or
  - a full prompted disclosure within the required time.

Giving advice to clients

Considerations of accountants	Factors relating to client to consider
- Know the Professional Code of Ethics. - Know your client – fact find. - Best advice – advice must be suitable. - Best execution – obtain best price. - Switching – avoid unnecessary transactions. - Key features – explain why course of action recommended.	- Personal objectives. - Current position. - Dependants. - Age. - Risk acceptable. - Tax status. - Tax efficiency. - Liquidity.

Personal financial management

Individuals must balance the need for income on an on-going basis with investing for capital growth to be used to fund retirement.

Suitable investments will change during an individual's lifetime as lifestyle and income streams change.

Factors to consider when making investments:

- Income available after meeting current obligations.
- Desire to own home and method of financing.
- Need to fund children's education.
- Responsibility to support parents.
- Required lifestyle on retirement.
- Desire to leave an inheritance to children.
- Need to ensure some investments are readily realisable to fund immediate unforeseen demands.
- Likelihood of receiving an inheritance.
- Attitude to risk.

Key investment products

Consider features of different investments to determine if they meet the needs of the client.

	IT free	CGT free	Risk	Liquidity	Income/ capital growth
Bank/ B Soc a/cs	x	N/A	L	L_1	I
NS&I	x	N/A	RF	L_1	I
NS&I savings certificates	3	3	RF	L_2	I
Premium bonds	3	3	RF	L_1	–
Qualifying life assurance policies	3	3	L	L_3	C
EIS and SEIS scheme	Tax relief on investment but income taxable	3	VH	L_3	C
VCT scheme	Tax relief on investment and dividends tax-free	3	H	L_1	C

	IT free	CGT free	Risk	Liquidity	Income/capital growth
Pension schemes (Tax relief on payments)	3	3	M	L_3	C
QCBs	x	3	M	L_1	C/I
Gilts	x	3	L	L_1	I
Land and buildings	x	x	M	L_3	C/I
REITs and unit trusts	x	x	M	L_1	C/I
Quoted shares/securities	x	x	M/H	L_1	C/I
Unquoted shares/securities	x	x	VH	L_3	C/I
Individual savings accounts	3	3	L/M	L_1	C/I

Key

I	Income	H	High risk
C	Capital growth	VH	Very high risk
x	Chargeable	L_1	Immediate access
3	Tax-free	L_2	Access possible but penalty
L	Low risk	L_3	Non-liquid
M	Medium risk	RF	Risk-free
		N/A	Not applicable

Tax efficient investment schemes

Special tax relief to encourage investment by individuals in riskier small companies.

	EIS	SEIS	VCT
Qualifying Individual	• Subscribes in cash • New ordinary shares • Qualifying company • Own ≤ 30% of ordinary share capital		• Subscribes • Newly issued shares
	• Not employee or director • Independent of company prior to first issue	• Not current employee (can be director or previous employee)	
Investment by individual	• Max £1 million p.a.	• Max £200,000 p.a.	• Max £200,000 p.a.
Retention period for IT relief	• 3 years • IT relief withdrawn if sold within 3 years		• 5 years • IT relief withdrawn if sold within 5 years
IT relief: Deduct from IT liability	• % of amount subscribed: = 30%	• % of amount subscribed: = 50%	• % of amount subscribed: = 30%

Carryback amount to previous year	• Any amount invested, but cannot get relief on more than £1 million in any one tax year	• Any amount invested, but cannot get relief on more than £200,000 in any one tax year	• No carryback
CGT on disposal	• Gain – Exempt if held ⩾ 3 yrs • Loss – Allowable – can convert into IT loss		• No gain or loss whenever sold
Reinvestment relief	• Gain on any chargeable asset = deferred subject to conditions • Gain crystallises when EIS shares disposed of or investor/spouse/civil partner emigrates < 3 years	• Up to a maximum of 50% of gain on any chargeable asset = exempt subject to conditions • Relief withdrawn if SEIS shares sold < 3 years	• No relief
IHT – BPR	• 100% if owned ⩾ 2 yrs		• No BPR
Dividends	• Taxable		• Tax-free on investment within annual limit

Ethics, personal financial management and self-assessment

Exam focus

Exam kit questions on this area:

Section A questions
- Pippin

Section B questions
- Pescara
- Tomas and Ines
- Luis

EIS reinvestment relief

- Individual:
  - disposes of any asset
  - subscribes for qualifying shares in EIS scheme
  - between 1 year before and 3 years after gain.
- Relief is lowest of:
  (1) the gain
  (2) amount subscribed for EIS shares
  (3) any smaller amount chosen.
- Individual must be resident in UK when gain realised and on reinvestment.
- Gain deferred until:
  - the disposal of the EIS shares by the investor, spouse / civil partner, or
  - the investor or spouse / civil partner (after a previous NGNL transfer) becomes non-UK resident (e.g. emigrates abroad) within 3 years of the issue of shares.
- Claim within 5 years from 31 January following the end of the tax year in which the disposal occurred.
- For 2024/25 disposals by 31 January 2031.
- Planning point:
  - choose to claim an amount of relief so that remaining gain is equal to the AEA and any available losses
  - work backwards in CGT pro forma to calculate amount of claim required.

If the asset qualifies for BADR a claim can be made such that gain is taxed in the year of disposal at 10%.

If a claim is not made the gain deferred will be taxed at the appropriate rate in force when it becomes chargeable.

If a gain deferred was entitled to BADR at the point of deferral, it will still be taxed at 10% when it becomes chargeable.

Exam focus

Exam kit questions on this area:

Section A questions
- Pippin

Section B questions
- Luis

SEIS reinvestment relief

- If an individual:
  - disposes of any chargeable asset, and
  - reinvests in qualifying SEIS shares, which
  - qualify for SEIS income tax (IT) relief

  some of the gain arising = **exempt** CGT.
- Any remaining gain is taxable in the normal way.

- Maximum SEIS exemption
  = **50% of the lower of the**
  (i) gain
  (ii) amount reinvested

  (**Maximum CGT exemption = £100,000** as maximum that can qualify for IT relief = £200,000).
- Relief = flexible, can claim any amount up to the maximum.
- Claim = same as EIS claim:

  For 2024/25 = by 31 January 2031.
- Planning point:
  - as for EIS relief: leave remaining gain equal to AEA and any available losses.

- Withdrawal of relief:
  - If the disposal within three years is:

	Not at arm's length	At arm's length
IT relief withdrawn	All	Lower of: • All • (50% x SP received)
CGT relief withdrawn	All	= $\dfrac{\text{Amount of IT relief withdrawn (above)}}{\text{Original IT relief given}}$ x Gain

Exam focus

Exam Kit questions on this area:

Section B questions

- Pescara

Key Point

There is no reinvestment relief for VCT investments.

Sources of finance

Personal

Mortgage
- lowest interest rate (cheap)
- longest term – secured on house.

Secured loan
- cheap, can be long term.

Unsecured loan
- more expensive
- normally < 5 yrs.

Hire purchase
- more expensive
- normally 1 – 5 yrs.

Overdraft
- expensive, short term, repayable on demand.

Credit cards
- most expensive (except zero percent cards).

Business

Equity
- does not need to be repaid
- dividends can vary each year, not tax deductible
- outside influence
- e.g. share issue, EIS and VCT schemes

Debt
- must be repaid
- interest payments fixed, but tax deductible.

Long term debt
- for purchase of assets, provision of working capital
- e.g. term loan, mortgage, debenture.

Short term debt
- e.g. overdraft, trade credit, debt factoring.

Chapter 10

Self-assessment

Filing for 2024/25 returns

- Later of:
  - 31 October 2025 (paper return)
  - 31 January 2026 (electronic return)
  - Three months after issue of the notice to file a return.
- Fixed and tax-geared penalties may apply for late filing (later in chapter).

Notification of chargeability

- Must notify HMRC of income or chargeable gains on which tax is due
  - Within 6 months of end of tax year in which the liability arises
  - i.e. by 5 October 2025 for 2024/25.
- Standard penalty may apply for failure to notify of chargeability (later in chapter).

Amendments to the return
- HMRC can amend return < 9 months of the actual filing date.
- Taxpayer can amend < 12 months of the 31 January filing date.

Determination of tax
- Issued by HMRC when a return is not filed by the 31 January filing date.
- Can be issued by HMRC within 3 years from the filing date (i.e. by 31 January 2029 for 2024/25 tax return).
- Assessment = replaced by the actual self-assessment return when it is submitted.

Records

Business records
- A business must keep records of:
  - all receipts and expenses
  - all goods purchased and sold
  - all supporting documents relating to the transactions of the business, such as accounts, books, contracts, vouchers.
- Self-employed taxpayers must retain all their records (not just business records) for five years after the 31 January filing date.
For 2024/25 = until 31 January 2031.

Other records
- Other taxpayers should keep evidence of income received.
- Must normally be retained for 12 months after the 31 January filing date.
  For 2024/25 = until 31 January 2027.

Penalty
- A fixed penalty of up to £3,000 may be charged for failure to keep or retain adequate records.

Payment dates for 2024/25

Payments on account (POAs)
- 31 January 2025.
- 31 July 2025.

Balancing payment
- 31 January 2026.

POAs = half previous year's tax payable by self-assessment and class 4 NIC (relevant amount)

- No POA if:
  - relevant amount for previous year is ≤ £1,000, or
  - more than 80% of the assessed tax (i.e. income tax and class 4 NIC) of the previous year was collected at source.

Late payment interest

Charged on:
- all late payments of tax
- at a daily rate
- runs from: due date
- to: date of payment

Repayment interest

HMRC pays interest on overpaid tax
- from: later of
  - date tax due, or
  - date HMRC received tax
- to: date of repayment

Exam focus

Exam kit questions on this area:
Section A questions
- Ray, Shanira and Kelly

Section B questions
- Ash

Standard penalties

Applies in two circumstances:
- Submission of incorrect returns
  - All taxes.
- Failure to notify liability to tax
  - Income tax, CGT, Corporation tax, VAT and NIC.
- Penalty = % of potential lost revenue.
- Depends on the behaviour of the taxpayer.

Taxpayer behaviour	Maximum penalty	Minimum penalty – unprompted disclosure	Minimum penalty – prompted disclosure
Deliberate and concealed	100%	30%	50%
Deliberate but not concealed	70%	20%	35%
Careless	30%	0%	15%

- The standard penalty table is available in the tax rates and allowances provided in the examination.

Ethics, personal financial management and self-assessment

- Penalties may be reduced at HMRC discretion, where the taxpayer informs HMRC
  - larger reductions for unprompted disclosure.

- Minimum penalties apply and vary based on:
  - the taxpayer's behaviour, and
  - whether disclosure is prompted or unprompted.
- An unprompted disclosure
  = where the taxpayer informs HMRC when there is no reason to believe HMRC have or are about to discover the error.
- Taxpayer can appeal against a standard penalty.

Other penalties relating to individuals

Offence	Penalty
Late filing of self-assessment tax return	
• filed after due date	£100 fixed penalty
Additional penalties:	
• filed 3 months late	Daily penalties of £10 per day (maximum of 90 days) in addition to £100 fixed penalty
• filed 6 months late	5% of tax due (minimum £300) plus above penalties
• more than 12 months after filing date where withholding information was:	The penalties above plus:
– not deliberate	Additional 5% of tax due (minimum £300)
– deliberate but no concealment	70% of tax due (minimum £300)
– deliberate with concealment	100% of tax due (minimum £300)

Ethics, personal financial management and self-assessment

Offence	Penalty
Late payment of tax • Paid > 1 month late • Paid > 6 months late • Paid > 12 months late	5% of tax due Additional 5% Additional 5% Applies to balancing payment only (not POAs)
Fraud or negligence on claiming reduced POAs	£ POAs if claim not made X Less: POAs actually paid (X) X
Failure to keep and retain required records	Up to £3,000 per year of assessment

Note that 'tax' for an individual will include income tax, capital gains tax and NIC.

HMRC compliance checks

- HMRC has the right to enquire into the completeness and accuracy of any return.
- Must issue written notice before commencing a compliance check (enquiry)
  - within 12 months of the date the return is actually filed.
- On completion of a compliance check, HMRC must send the taxpayer a completion notice:
  - either stating no amendment required, or
  - amending the taxpayer's self-assessment.
- Taxpayer has 30 days to appeal against HMRC's amendment.

Discovery assessments

- HMRC can raise a discovery assessment if they discover an inaccuracy in the return within

	Time from end of tax year	For 2024/25
Basic time limit	4 years	5 April 2029
Careless error	6 years	5 April 2031
Deliberate error	20 years	5 April 2045

Ethics, personal financial management and self-assessment

Information and inspection powers

- Covers income tax, capital gains tax, corporation tax, VAT and PAYE.
- HMRC can request information from taxpayers
  - by a written information notice.
- Requests to third parties for information must normally
  - be agreed by the taxpayer, or
  - approved by the first-tier tribunal.
- HMRC also has powers to
  - enter and inspect a taxpayer's business premises
  - in order to inspect business records and assets.

Appeals to resolve disputes with HMRC

- Taxpayer can appeal against a decision made by HMRC
  - in writing
  - within 30 days of the disputed decision.
- They can proceed in one of two ways:
  - request a review by another HMRC officer, or
  - refer case to an independent Tax Tribunal.

Tax Tribunals

Two tiers (layers) of Tax Tribunal system:
- First-tier Tribunal, and
- Upper Tribunal.

The First-tier Tribunal deals with:
- Default paper cases:
  - simple appeals (e.g. against a fixed penalty)
  - usually no hearing provided both sides agree.
- Basic cases:
  - straightforward appeals
  - minimal exchange of paperwork
  - a short hearing.
- Standard cases:
  - more detailed consideration of issues
  - more formal hearing.
- Complex cases:
  - may be heard by the First Tier
  - however usually heard by Upper Tribunal.

The Upper Tribunal will deal with:
- Complex cases
  - requiring detailed specialist knowledge
  - a formal hearing.

Hearings are held in public and decisions are published.

A decision of the Upper Tribunal:
- may be appealed to the Court of Appeal
- but only on grounds of a point of law.

chapter 11

Income tax – overview and investment income

In this chapter

- Income tax pro forma.
- Rates of income tax.
- Married couples and civil partners.
- Exempt income.
- Property income.
- Rent-a-room relief.
- Furnished holiday accommodation.
- Real estate investment trusts.

Income tax – overview and investment income

Exam focus

The computation of income tax is likely to feature throughout the examination.

Income from property is another key topic covered in this chapter.

It is also important to understand the marginal effect of transactions (i.e. the additional income tax payable as a result of receiving additional income, or the income tax savings where income is reduced).

Exam focus

The income tax computation is essential knowledge.

Use the following pro forma to gain easy marks on this aspect of the examination.

Income tax pro forma

Income tax computation – 2024/25

	£
Total income	x
Less: Reliefs	(x)
Net income	x
Less: Personal allowance	(x)
Taxable income	x

Income tax – analyse income

	Non-savings	Savings	Dividend
Basic rate band (first £37,700)	20%	20%	8.75%
Higher rate band (£37,701 – £125,140)	40%	40%	33.75%
Additional rate band (over £125,140)	45%	45%	39.35%

Income tax payable

	£
Total income tax (per rates)	x
Less: Tax reducers	(x)
Income tax liability	x
Less: Tax credits/PAYE	(x)
Payments on account	(x)
Income tax payable/(repayable)	x/(x)

Notes:

(1) If savings income falls into the first £5,000 of taxable income it is taxed at 0% (not 20%).

(2) A savings income nil rate band of £1,000/£500 is available to basic/higher rate taxpayers respectively – The savings income nil rate band is not available to additional rate taxpayers.

(3) All taxpayers are entitled to a £500 dividend nil rate band.

(4) Overseas income assessed under the remittance basis will be subject to income tax at the non-savings income rates. The savings and dividend nil rate bands and the lower rates applicable to dividends will not be available.

Key Point

Extend the basic rate and higher rate bands if a taxpayer makes payments into a personal pension scheme.

Exam focus

Section A questions
- Ziti
- Pippin
- Gail and Brad
- Jeg Ltd Group

Section B questions
- Shuttelle
- Pinto
- Cate and Ravi
- Traiste Ltd

Reliefs

- Interest on qualifying loans – paid gross
- Loss reliefs
- Maximum deduction from total income = greater of
  - £50,000
  - 25% x adjusted total income (ATI)
- Therefore the restriction will be £50,000 unless ATI exceeds £200,000
- ATI is calculated as:

	£
Total income	X
Less: Gross PPCs	(X)
ATI	X

Exam focus

The maximum restriction is more likely to be examined in the context of loss relief (Chapter 16)

Personal allowance (PA)

- Available to all individuals
- £12,570 for 2024/25
- Deducted from net income to give taxable income
- Transferable amount £1,260 (later in chapter)
- Lost if not used in the year

Chapter 11

Reduction of PA – higher rate taxpayers

- If Adjusted net income (ANI) > £100,000:
  - reduce PA by:
    $50\% \times$ (ANI – £100,000)
- If ANI > £125,140:
  - no PA
- Effective rate of tax on income between £100,000 to £125,140: 60%
- ANI is calculated as:

	£
Net income per IT comp	x
Less: Gross PPCs	(x)
ANI	x

Exam focus

Exam kit questions on this area:

Section B questions

- Shuttelle
- Cate and Ravi

Marriage Allowance

- A spouse or civil partner can elect to transfer a fixed amount of the PA to the other spouse/civil partner.
- This is known as the marriage allowance (MA).
- Neither spouse/civil partner may be a higher or additional rate taxpayer.

Method:

- The fixed amount of PA to transfer: = £1,260 for 2024/25.
- There is no provision for transferring less than this amount.
- Relief is given by reducing the recipient's income tax liability by a maximum of £252 (i.e. £1,260 × 20% BR income tax).

Tax reducers

- EIS, SEIS and VCT relief = 30%/50%/30%
- DTR = Lower of UK and overseas tax

Rates of income tax

- Income tax rate bands apply to the different types of income in the following order:
  1. non-savings income
  2. savings income
  3. dividend income
- To maximise tax relief in most cases offset PA and reliefs against income in the same order as above.
- In some circumstances it is beneficial to offset the PA in a different order e.g. offset against dividend income first to avoid wasting the savings starting rate or nil rate band.

Income

Non-savings income:
- Employment income
- Trading income
- Property income
- Pension income
- Trust income: discretionary, or property income from an IIP trust.

Savings income:
- Interest received net of (20%) tax: interest from an IIP trust, unquoted loan stock issued by UK resident companies.
- Interest received gross: NS&I accounts, gilts, treasury stock, exchequer stock, quoted loan stock issued by UK resident companies, bank and building societies.

Dividend income:
- This includes overseas dividends for all UK resident individuals.

Married couples and civil partners

Joint income
- Applies to married couples and civil partnerships.
- The income arising from assets (except shares in close companies) held jointly by spouses/civil partners is normally split 50:50.
- An election is available to split the income according to beneficial ownership.
- The election cannot be made for joint bank or building society accounts.

Parental dispositions
- Income earned by a child from a parental disposition = taxed on the parent if the gross income received in the tax year exceeds £100 p.a.

Exempt income

- Interest on:
  - NS&I Savings Certificates
  - Save As You Earn (SAYE) share save accounts
  - Repayment interest (interest on tax repayments).
- Dividends received on shares from venture capital trusts (VCTs).
- Scholarships and educational grants.
- Prizes and winnings (i.e. premium bonds, betting).
- Statutory redundancy pay and the first £30,000 of compensation received for loss of employment.
- Certain state benefits (Child benefit, Universal credit).
- Income from individual savings account (ISAs).
- On death of a spouse/civil partner:
  - value of ISAs held at death = available as additional ISA allowance for surviving spouse/civil partner.

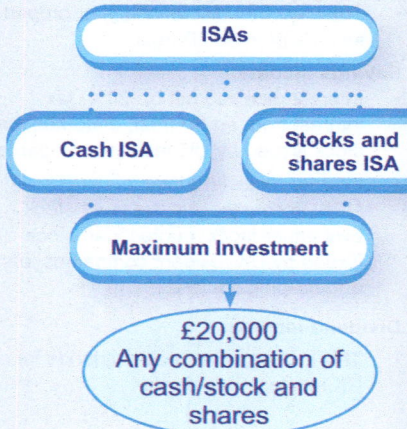

Property income

- Taxes income from land and property.
- Taxable income calculated using trading income rules; wholly and exclusively test.
- Assessed on a cash basis.
- Accruals basis is compulsory if gross annual rent > £150,000 or can elect to use accruals basis.
- Taxed as other income at:
  - 20%, 40% or 45%.
- Additional points re expenses:
  - interest paid = allowable deduction for individuals subject to special rules (later in chapter)
  - replacement furniture relief for the cost of replacing furnishings.
- Property income losses
  - for individuals, can only be carried forward against future UK property income.

Pro forma – property income

	£
Rent received in the tax year	X
Plus: Rental income portion of short lease premiums received in tax year (later in chapter)	A
Less: Allowable expenses	(X)
Profit / (loss)	X/(X)

Financing costs

- Tax relief restricted to basic rate.
- Applies to finance costs relating to loans to buy or improve residential property.
  - No finance costs deductible from property income.
  - Tax relief for all finance costs given at basic rate (20%) by deduction from income tax liability.
- Note: No restrictions for:
  - companies
  - loans relating to furnished holiday accommodation
  - loans relating to non-residential properites.

Premium for granting short leases only

Income element is calculated as:

	£
Premium	X
Less: 2% × premium × (n – 1)	(X)
Income element	A

Alternative calculation:

$$A = \text{Premium} \times \frac{51 - n}{50}$$

Where n = no. of years of lease

Rent-a-room relief

- Furnished room in a main domestic residence.
- Gross rents ≤ £7,500
  - exempt, unless elect for loss.
- Gross rents > £7,500
  - normal property income calculation
  - unless elect for excess over £7,500 to be taxed (with no deduction for expenses).

Furnished holiday accommodation (FHA)

- Assessed as property income but:
  - treat as arising from a single and separate trade.
- Advantages:
  - business asset for CGT rollover relief, gift holdover relief and BADR
  - relevant earnings for pensions relief
  - finance costs fully deductible
  - deduction available for all P&M, including furniture, if using cash basis
  - capital allowances available for P&M, including furniture, if using accruals basis
  - 100% of finance costs deductible from FHA income.

- Losses:
  - can only be set against profits from the same FHA business
  - UK FHA losses can only be set against UK FHA profits
  - EEA FHA losses can only be set against EEA FHA profits
  - firstly offset in the same year
  - then carry forward.
- Conditions:
  - situated in UK or EEA
  - let furnished on commercial basis
  - available to let ≥ 210 days/tax year
  - actually let ≥ 105 days/tax year
  - if own more than one property, averaging is available to satisfy the 105 day rule
  - not let for periods of 'long term occupation' (occupied by same person > 31 consecutive days) in excess of 155 days in a 12-month period.

Exam focus

Exam kit questions on this area:

Section B questions

- Pedro

Real estate investment trusts (REITs)

- Quoted property investment trust.
- Dividends received by individual from REIT:
  - treated as property income
  - received net of 20% tax.

chapter

12

Employment income – income tax and national insurance

In this chapter

- Employment income – pro forma.
- Benefits summary.
- Vehicle benefits.
- Living accommodation.
- Beneficial loans.
- Use of assets.
- Gift of assets.
- Share options – tax treatment.
- Tax advantaged schemes.
- Lump sum payments.
- National insurance.

Employment income – income tax and national insurance

Exam focus

Employment is a particularly important area.

Skills required may vary from performing the basic calculation of employee benefits to higher skills. For example, making decisions between whether an employee should accept a company car or own and run a car personally and take a cash alternative from the business instead.

You may also be required to express an opinion on whether an individual, given a particular scenario, is likely to be treated as self-employed or as an employee.

Employment income – pro forma

	£	£
Salary		x
Bonus/Commission		x
Benefits		x
Gross earnings		x
Less: Allowable expenses (Covered overleaf)		(x)
Add: Redundancy payment	x	
Add: Non-tax advantaged share option plan on exercise	x	
Less: Exempt portion (First £30,000 of non-contractual redundancy is tax-free)	(x)	
		x
Employment income		x

Chapter 12

Exam focus

Exam kit questions on this area:

Section B questions
- Shuttelle
- Cate and Ravi
- Methley Ltd
- Traiste Ltd
- Damiana plc
- Jessica
- Demeter
- Samphire Ltd and Kelp Ltd

Allowable expenses

- Contributions to employer's occupational pension scheme.
- Subscriptions to professional bodies.
- Charitable donations under a payroll deduction scheme.
- Travel, subsistence and entertaining incurred wholly, exclusively and necessarily in the performance of the office or employment (Note).
- Cost of partnership shares acquired in a share incentive plan (SIP).
- Deficit on mileage allowance (AMAP).

Note: Travel and related expenses
- Not travel from home to permanent workplace.
- Travel from home to a temporary workplace is allowed if the placement is expected to last less than 2 years.

Benefits summary

Taxable benefits	Exempt benefits
General rule: Taxed on cost to employer (marginal cost if 'in house' benefit) **Special rules:** Non-cash vouchers – cost to employer Accommodation (later in chapter) Company cars/vans/fuel Beneficial loans Gift and use of assets Accommodation (later in chapter)	• Job-related accommodation • Subsidised canteen (unless part of salary sacrifice scheme) • Up to £6 per week towards additional household costs where the employee works from home • Employer pension contributions • Workplace parking • Relocation expenses ≤ £8,000 • Overnight subsistence • Mobile phone (one) • Workplace nurseries • Annual party ≤ £150 per person per annum • Eye care tests • Cheap loans ≤ £10,000 • AMAPs • Recommended medical treatment assisting return to work (up to £500 per employee per tax year)

Exam focus

Points frequently examined:

- employee contributions
  - deduct amounts paid in tax year from benefit
  - but note special rules for car: capital contributions (max £5,000) and fuel contributions (not allowable).
- where the benefit is wholly and exclusively for employment
  - calculate benefit and deduct expense claim.
- benefits not available for part of year
  - time apportion.

Approved mileage allowance payments (AMAPs)

If employee uses own car, van, motorcycle or bicycle for business purposes:

AMAPs = tax-free

If mileage allowance received > AMAP:

Excess = taxable benefit

If mileage allowance received < AMAP:

Shortfall = allowable deduction from employment income

Passenger payments (if provided) for taking colleagues on same business trip:

- tax-free if up to statutory limit (5p per passenger)
- no deduction for a shortfall.

Exam focus

- The AMAP rates for cars and vans will be provided in the tax rates and allowances (but not the passenger or other rates).

Exam focus

Exam kit questions on this area:

Section B questions

- Hyssop Ltd
- Morice and Babeen plc

Vehicle benefits

VEHICLE BENEFITS

Where employer provides vehicle used for private purposes by employee.

Car benefit

Basic car benefit:

List price $\times$ % $\times \frac{n}{12}$

- list price, including extras
- employee capital contribution deductible (max £5,000)
- benefit reduced if unavailable > 30 days
- benefit includes all running costs except private fuel
- n = number of months car available

Private fuel

£27,800 $\times$ % $\times \frac{n}{12}$

- % based on car percentage
- Employee contributions ignored unless reimburses private fuel in full

Van benefit

- £3,960 p.a. for use of van
- £757 p.a. for private fuel
- There is no van benefit or fuel benefit for zero-emission vans.
- Time apportion if unavailable > 30 days

Appropriate %

The percentage used to calculate the car benefit depends on CO_2 emissions and electric range.

CO_2 emissions	Electric range (miles)	Appropriate %
0	N/A	2%
1-50g/km	>130	2%
1-50g/km	70-129	5%
1-50g/km	40-69	8%
1-50g/km	30-39	12%
1-50g/km	<30	14%
51g/km - 54g/km		15%
55g/km or more		16%: increase by 1% for every complete 5 grams above 55 g/km (max 37%)
Diesel: extra charge (not for RDE2 cars)		4% (max 37%)

Living accommodation

Benefit	Amount taxable	Job-related accommodation
Basic charge	Higher of: • Annual value • Rent paid by employer	Exempt
Expensive accommodation charge (where employer owns property and cost is > £75,000)	(Cost – £75,000) × ORI ORI = official rate of interest (provided in the exam)	Exempt
Ancillary services:		
• Use of furniture	20% × market value when first provided	Same as for non-job related accommodation except: Maximum total benefit restricted to 10% of other employment income
• Living expenses (e.g. heating, electricity, decorating)	Cost to employer	
• Council tax	Cost to employer	No charge

Chapter 12

Key Point

- Where the employer rents the accommodation there can never be an expensive accommodation charge.
- For the expensive accommodation charge:

    Cost = Acquisition cost of the property **plus** capital improvements up to the **start** of the tax year.

    If the property is occupied by the employee more than 6 years after it was acquired by the employer:

    - substitute the acquisition cost with the market value at the date the property was first occupied.

Job-related accommodation

Definition

Accommodation which is:

- necessary for proper performance of employee's duties, or
- provided for the better performance of duties and it is customary to provide such accommodation, or
- provided as part of special security arrangements because of a specific threat to the employee's security.

Exam focus

Exam kit questions on this area:

Section B questions

- Shuttelle
- Demeter
- Dent Ltd

Employment income – income tax and national insurance

Beneficial loans

Where an interest-free/subsidised loan made to employee:

	£
Capital (below)	
× official rate of interest (ORI)	X
Less: Interest actually paid	(X)
Taxable benefit	X

- ORI = 2.25% for June 2025 to March 2026 exam sittings (given in tax tables)

- Two methods of calculation of capital:
  - Average method:

    $$\frac{\text{Opening balance} + \text{Closing balance}}{2} = \text{average capital}$$

  - Precise method:
    calculated each month on balance outstanding

- Either taxpayer or HMRC can elect for precise method to be used.

Exceptions

- No benefit if:
  - total loans outstanding at any time in the tax year is ≤ £10,000, or
  - loans made on ordinary commercial terms (i.e. same terms as to public)

Exam focus

- The benefit should be calculated using both methods in the examination unless the question states otherwise.

Exam kit questions on this area:

Section B questions

- Morice and Babeen plc

Use of assets

- Benefit:
  20% × MV when first made available
- 20% rule does not apply to private use of cars, vans and accommodation provided by employer.

Gift of assets

New asset:
Benefit = cost to employer.

Used asset:

- Benefit is greater of:

Method 1

	£
– Market value at time of transfer	X
Less: Amount paid by employee	(X)
	X

and

Method 2

– Market value when first used	X
Less: Amount charged as benefit over period of use	(X)
Less: Amount paid by employee	(X)
	X

- These rules do not apply to transfer of:
  - a used car or van
  - bicycles provided for work.

  The benefit in this instance
  = Method 1

Share options – tax treatment

	Non-tax advantaged (unapproved)	Tax advantaged (approved)
Grant of option	No tax	No tax
Exercise of options (i.e. buy shares)	Income tax and NIC Collected under PAYE immediately Chargeable to income tax: 　　　　　　　　　　　　　£ MV @ exercise date　　　　x Less: 　Cost of option　　　　　(x) 　Cost of shares　　　　　(x) Employment income　　　　x	No tax
Sale of shares	CGT　　　　　　　　　　　£ Proceeds　　　　　　　　　x Less: Cost of shares　　　(x) Chargeable gain　　　　　x Cost of shares = MV when exercised	CGT　　　　　　　　　　　£ Proceeds　　　　　　　　　x Less: Cost of shares　　　(x) Chargeable gain　　　　　x Cost of shares = Exercise price

Notes

(1) Class 1 NIC will be payable by both the employee and employer if the shares are quoted. No NIC will be payable if the shares are unquoted.

(2) The gain is taxed at 0%, 10%, or 20% depending on the availability of the AEA, BADR and level of taxable income.

(3) BADR will only be available if:
- the employee owns at least 5% shareholding of the company
- for the 2 years prior to sale.

Except for EMI shares, where:
- the 2 years ownership commences at the date the option is granted, and
- there is no 5% holding requirement.

Exam focus

Exam kit questions on this area:

Section B questions
- Damiana plc
- Demeter
- Rod

Tax advantaged schemes

Tax advantaged share option schemes

	CSOP	EMI	SAYE
Participation	Employer chooses	Employer chooses	All employees
Maximum value	£60,000 per employee	£250,000 per employee Scheme max £3m	£500 per month
Exercise period	3 – 10 years	Up to 10 years	3 or 5 years
Issue price	MV	Issue at MV to avoid IT charge	Not < 80% of MV
Base cost of shares for CGT	Price paid	Price paid plus discount taxed as income on exercise (if any)	Price paid
Other	If own > 30% of company = excluded from the scheme	Gross assets ≤ £30m Employees < 250 BADR period of ownership runs from date of grant (not date shares acquired) and no need to own ≥ 5% of OSC	

Share incentive plan (SIP)

Participation	All employees
Awarded free shares	Max £3,600 per year
Purchase partnership shares	Max = lower of: • £1,800, and • 10% salary Cost = allowable deduction against employment income
Awarded matching shares	Max 2 per partnership share
Dividends	Tax-free if invested in further shares

Holding period	• 5 years – IT and NIC free
	• If 3-5 years IT and NIC on lower of:
	  – initial value at the shares
	  – Value at the date of withdrawal
	• If less than 3 years
	  IT and NIC on value of the shares at the time when they cease to be held in the plan

Base cost of shares	MV when removed from plan

Employment income – income tax and national insurance

Exam focus

In the examination you may be required to recommend a suitable tax advantaged share scheme based on the facts in a particular situation.

Use the following factors to assist in deciding the most appropriate option:

- participants – open to all/selective scheme
- share award vs share option scheme
- financial limits – amount to be awarded
- size of company – EMI only available to smaller companies
- holding period for shares/options.

Exam focus

Exam kit questions on this area:

Section A questions
- Olma and Hogan

Section B questions
- Morice and Babeen plc
- Klubb plc
- Methley Ltd
- Demeter
- Rod
- Yacon Ltd and Daikon

Lump sum payments

- generally associated with termination.
- but may be used as an incentive to attract an employee.

Three types:

Wholly exempt	Fully taxable	First £30,000 exempt
• Payments for death, injury and disability • Statutory redundancy pay • Approved lump sum on retirement	• Pay in lieu of notice • Reward for past or future services	• Genuine ex-gratia payments for loss of office (below)

Termination payments on loss of office

- If contractual = taxable
- If non-contractual / ex-gratia = first £30,000 exempt
  - £30,000 includes statutory redundancy pay
- Restrictive covenants (i.e. restraint of trade) = fully taxable.

Taxable amounts

- Taxed in year of receipt
- Paid before P45 = Paid net of PAYE
- Paid after P45 = Paid net of marginal rate income tax
- Taxed as top slice of income (after dividends)
- No employee NICs on non-contractual payment, but employer pays class 1A NICs on excess above £30,000.

Exam focus

Exam kit questions on this area:
Section B questions

- Traiste Ltd
- Jessica

National insurance

Employees

Employee class 1

- Employees pay class 1 NICs on their 'cash earnings'.
- Cash earnings includes:
  - any remuneration derived from employment and paid in money
  - vouchers exchangeable for cash or non-cash items
  - reimbursement of cost of travel between home and work.
- Cash earnings does not include:
  - exempt employment benefits
  - most non-cash benefits
  - reimbursement of business expenses
  - mileage allowance ≤ 45p per mile.
- Payable by all employees
  - aged 16 to state pension age.
- Payable at 8% on earnings between £12,570 and £50,270.
- Payable at 2% on earnings above £50,270.
- Contributions are collected by the employer through the PAYE scheme.

Employers

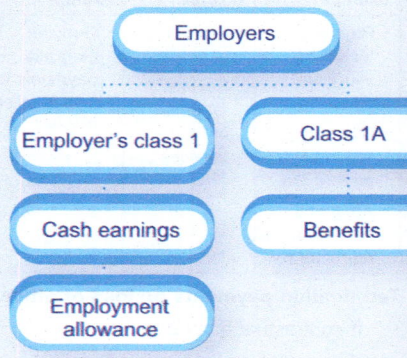

Employer's class 1

- Cost borne by employer.
- Allowable trading expense for tax purposes.
- Rate of 13.8% on earnings over £9,100 per annum.
- Paid on 'cash earnings', as for employee class 1.
- Paid in respect of employees aged ≥ 16.
- Employment allowance available.
- Payable with employee class 1 contributions through PAYE system.
- Payable on 22nd of the next month (electronic payments), or 19th of the next month if not paid electronically.

Employment allowance

- Up to £5,000 p.a. allowance.
- Deducted from employer's class 1 NICs only.
- Only available if employer's class 1 NICs < £100,000 in previous tax year.
- Not available where a director is the company's only employee paid over £9,100.
- Claimed though the PAYE system.

Class 1A

- Payable by the employer only.
- Rate of 13.8% on taxable benefits provided to the employee.
- Payable by 22 July following the tax year if paid electronically) or 19 July (if not paid electronically).

Employment income – income tax and national insurance

chapter 13

Relief for pensions

In this chapter

- Pensions – overview.
- Types of pension schemes.
- Tax relief.
- Annual allowance.
- Benefits on retirement.

Relief for pensions

Exam focus

Individuals investing in a pension scheme can reduce their income tax liability at their highest marginal rate in the tax year in which they make the investment.

Questions may require you to:

- provide information regarding the rules about the maximum amount a person is permitted to invest in a pension scheme
- advise a client as to how much tax can be saved when investing in a pension scheme, and/or
- advise a client as to the maximum amount to invest in a particular tax year in order to maximise tax relief.

Pensions – overview

- Tax relief available for contributions by under 75 year olds into HMRC registered pension schemes.
- Scheme must satisfy conditions but these are not examinable.

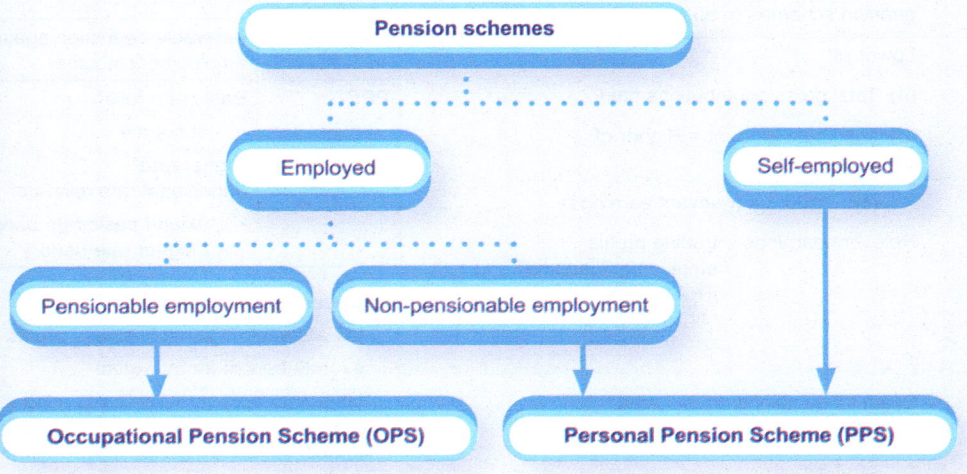

Relief for pensions

Tax relief

Tax relief available for contributions into pension schemes of up to:

Lower of:

(a) Total gross contributions paid

(b) Maximum amount = Higher of:

  (i) £3,600
  (ii) 100% × (relevant earnings).

Relevant earnings = trading profits,
employment income,
FHA income.

Exam focus

Exam kit questions on this area:

Section B questions

- Shuttelle
- Jessica

Method of relief

Employee contributions

OPS	Allowable deduction against employment income
PPS	Basic rate relief • at source Higher rate / additional rate relief • extend basic rate band / higher rate band

Employer contributions

- tax allowable against business profits
- exempt benefit for individual
- taken into account when calculating total contributions to be compared with the annual allowance (AA).

Annual allowance (AA)

- Where total contributions paid into pension schemes > the current year AA plus unused AA b/f:
  - a tax charge arises on the excess.
- The tax charge is:
  - taxed as the individual's top slice of income
  - paid through the self-assessment system.

Exam focus

In the examination:
- tax the excess last (i.e. after dividends) at non-savings rates.
- Unused AA b/f from the **previous three tax years** is taken into account:
  - can only be c/f if the individual was a member of a pension scheme for that tax year.

- The AA limit for three years prior to 2024/25 was:
  - 2023/24: £60,000
  - 2022/23: £40,000
  - 2021/22: £40,000
- Order of utilisation:
  - current year AA is used first
  - then earlier three years unused amount, on a FIFO basis.

Exam focus

Exam kit questions on this area:

Section B questions
- Shuttelle
- Jessica
- Demeter
- Pedro

Relief for pensions

Restriction of annual allowance – high income individuals

- The annual allowance of £60,000 is gradually reduced for individuals with high income.
- The restriction applies to individuals with a 'threshold income' exceeding £200,000 and 'adjusted income' exceeding £260,000.
- The annual allowance is reduced by: (Adjusted income – £260,000) × 50%.
- The maximum reduction to the annual allowance is £50,000, meaning the minimum annual allowance is £10,000.

Threshold income

	£
Net income (from the income tax computation)	X
Less: Individual's **gross personal pension** contributions	(X)
Threshold income	X

Adjusted income

	£
Net income (from the income tax computation)	X
Plus: Individual **employee's occupational pension** contributions	X
Employer's contributions into any scheme for that individual	X
Adjusted income	X

If threshold income ≤ £200,000	The annual allowance for the tax year is £60,000 (no restriction).
If threshold income > £200,000 and adjusted income ≤ £260,000:	
If threshold income is > £200,000 and adjusted income > £260,000:	The annual allowance for the tax year must be reduced by (adjusted income − £260,000) × 50%.

Relief for pensions

Benefits on retirement

Pension fund grows tax-free

- Exempt income tax.
- Exempt capital gains tax.

Commencement of benefits

- Aged 55.
- Can continue to work and draw a pension.

Tax-free lump sum

- Maximum = 25% of value of fund.
- The balance of the fund can be withdrawn at any time.
- Withdrawals from the balance are subject to income tax at normal rates (20%, 40% or 45%).

Pension income

- Pension income = taxable earned income.
- On death – pension income and/or lump sums for dependants may be made.

chapter 14

Personal tax – overseas aspects

In this chapter

- Tax status.
- Domicile.
- Deemed domicile.
- Residence.
- Splitting tax year.
- Income tax.
- Capital gains tax.
- Inheritance tax.

Personal tax – overseas aspects

Exam focus

The overseas aspects of income tax, capital gains tax and inheritance tax can feature as part of a question.

You must be able to deal with situations involving individuals either coming to or leaving the UK and with all of the taxes involved.

Tax status

- How an individual is assessed to income tax and capital gains tax depends on the individual's:
  - Residency status, and,
  - Domicile.

Exam focus

You may be required to assess the residence or domicile position of an individual in a particular scenario. It is essential that you are familiar with these definitions.

Domicile

Definition

An individual's permanent home.

Domicile of origin:
- acquired at birth
- normally domicile of father.

Domicile of dependency
- up to the age of 16
- if father changes domicile, individual follows suit.

Domicile of choice

(e.g. where an individual emigrates to another country)
- need to demonstrate severed all ties with UK.

Deemed domicile

Definition

An individual can be deemed UK domiciled for IT and CGT purposes.

Long term residents
- UK resident for 15 of previous 20 tax years, unless not UK resident in any tax year after 5 April 2017.

Formerly domiciled residents
- Born in the UK, and
- UK domicile of origin, and
- UK resident in the tax year.

Exam focus

Exam kit questions on this area:

Section B questions
- Shutelle

Personal tax – overseas aspects

Residence

Definition

An individual will be resident in the tax year if the individual:

- does not meet one of the **automatic non-UK residence tests**, and
- meets one of the **automatic UK residence tests**, or
- meets one or more of the **sufficient ties tests**.

Exam focus

Exam kit questions on this area:

Section A questions
- Waverley and Set Ltd Group

Section B questions
- Pinto
- Mirtoon

Key Point

If an individual satisfies an automatic non-UK residence test and automatic UK residence test = non-UK resident.

Resident in UK?

Automatic non-UK residency tests

Individual in UK in **tax year** less than
- **16 days**, or
- **46 days** and not UK R in any of last 3 years, or
- **91 days** and works FT abroad

Automatic UK residency tests

Individual in UK at least:
- **183 days** in tax year, or
- **30 days** in tax year and only home in UK, or
- **365 days** continuously, some in tax year and work FT

Sufficient ties tests

1. Close family resident in UK – Spouse/Civil partner/minor child
2. Accommodation in UK – available 91 consecutive days in tax year
3. Substantive work in UK – 40 days
4. Days in UK in last two tax years – › 90 days in either year
5. Country tie – Most time spent in UK

Previously resident = UK R in one of last 3 years

Consider **all five** ties

Use tax tables in exam

Not previously resident = not UK R in any of last 3 years

Consider **first four** ties

Application of sufficient ties tests

Days spent in the UK	Previously resident	Not previously resident
Less than 16 days	Automatically **not** UK resident	Automatically **not** UK resident
16 to 45 days	Resident if: 4 UK ties (or more)	Automatically **not** UK resident
46 to 90 days	Resident if: 3 UK ties (or more)	Resident if: 4 UK ties
91 to 120 days	Resident if: 2 UK ties (or more)	Resident if: 3 UK ties (or more)
121 to 182 days	Resident if: 1 UK tie (or more)	Resident if: 2 UK ties (or more)
183 or more days	Automatically resident	Automatically resident

Note that this table will be provided in the tax rates and allowances.

Splitting tax year

Split year basis (SYB) can apply if individual = UK R in tax year under automatic tests or sufficent ties test.

- SYB = automatic if conditions satisfied
- Cannot disapply SYB

Key Point

- If non-UK R in the tax year
  - SYB cannot apply
  - Will be non-UK R for whole tax year

SPLITTING TAX YEAR

Leaving the UK

Individual must be
- UK resident in current year, and
- UK resident in previous year, and
- not UK resident in the following year

Individual leaves the UK and:
1. Begins working full time abroad
2. Accompanies partner working full time abroad
3. Ceases to have any UK home

Overseas part starts:

Date start work abroad

Later of date
– Joins partner
– Partner starts work abroad

Date have no UK home

Arriving in the UK

Individual must be
- UK resident in current year, and
- Not UK resident in previous year

Individual arrives in the UK and:
1. Acquires a UK home
2. Begins working full time in the UK for ≥ 365 days
3. Returns following a period when individual (or partner) worked full time overseas

UK part starts:

Date acquires UK home
Date start work in UK

Date individual (or partner) stops working overseas

Income tax

General rule:
- UK resident
  - Taxed on UK and overseas income.
- Non-resident
  - Taxed on UK income only
  - Personal allowance available against UK income for UK/EEA citizens.

Key Point

- All income arising in the UK is always subject to UK income tax irrespective of individual's status.
- A UK resident is always taxed on overseas income
  - the only issue is whether the individual is taxed on an arising or remittance basis.

Chapter 14

```
                    SOURCE OF INCOME
                   /                \
            UK income            Overseas income
                |              /        |         \
                |        R and D       NR in UK   R but ND
                |        in UK                    in UK
```

UK income
- Always taxable whatever the status of the individual
- **Arising basis**

R and D in UK
- Taxable
- **Arising basis**
- DTR available
- Personal allowances always available

NR in UK
- Not taxable
- **= Exempt**
- No DTR as no double taxation
- Personal allowances available **if** EEA, Isle of Man or Channel Islands citizen

R but ND in UK
- Taxable
- **Arising basis or Remittance basis?**
- (In next diagram)
- DTR available
- Personal allowances may be available (In next diagram)

Personal tax – overseas aspects

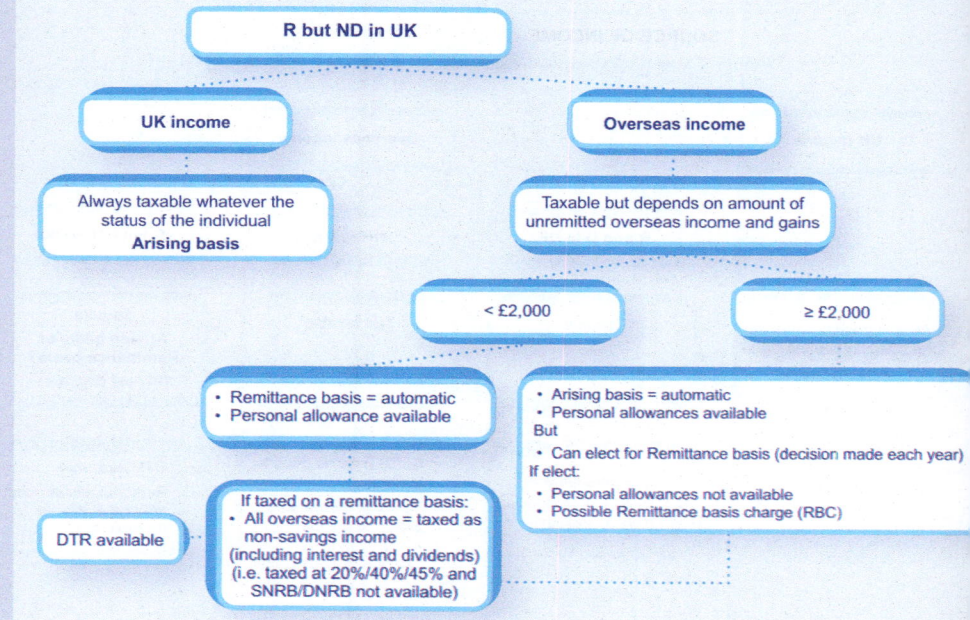

- The remittance basis will still be automatically available to deemed domiciled individuals whose unremitted overseas income and gains are under £2,000.

Exam focus

Exam kit questions on this area:

Section A questions
- Joe and Fiona
- Ray, Shanira and Kelly

Section B questions
- Shuttelle
- Pinto
- Methley Ltd
- Caden and Amahle

Remittance Basis Charge (RBC)

- Only levied if individual:
  - aged ≥ 18 years old
  - is not UK domiciled
  - is UK resident in current tax year
  - has been UK resident for 7 out of last 9 tax years
  - has total unremitted income and gains > £2,000, and
  - elects for the remittance basis to apply.
- Additional tax charge:

	if UK resident for
£30,000 p.a.	7 out of last 9 tax years
£60,000 p.a.	12 out of last 14 tax years

- Added to income tax liability.
- Paid under self-assessment.

Exam focus

Exam kit questions on this area:

Section A questions

- Joe and Fiona

Section B questions

- Shuttelle
- Methley Ltd

Double tax relief

> Deduct from the individual's income tax liability
> Lower of:
> - Overseas tax suffered
> - UK income tax on that source of overseas income

> UK income tax attributable to a source of overseas income
> = the reduction in the total income tax liability that would arise if that source of overseas income is excluded from taxable income

> To calculate UK income tax on overseas income:
> - Always treat overseas income as the 'top slice' of income type
> - Calculate total income tax **including** that source of overseas income
> - Calculate total income tax **without** that source of overseas income
> - Difference = UK income tax on that source income

> If more than one source of overseas income:
> - Need separate DTR calculation for each source of overseas income
> - Take out the source with the **highest rate of overseas tax** first

Exam focus

You may be asked to consider the tax position of:

- an individual coming to work in the UK, or
- a UK individual leaving the UK to work abroad.

Exam kit questions on this area:

Section B questions

- Mirtoon

Key Point

Individual comes to UK to take up employment

- Taxed under normal rules.
- UK residency position depends on intentions when arrive in UK.
- Tax position resulting from residency position:
  - Taxed on all UK source income on an arising basis regardless of residency status
  - Overseas income:
    Refer to earlier diagram.

Capital gains tax

- General rule:

Individual's status	Taxed on
R and domiciled in UK	Worldwide assets
Not R in UK, regardless of domicile	No liability on any assets (unless trading in UK, temporary absence abroad or UK property)
R in UK; but Not UK domiciled	UK gains – Arising basis Non UK gains – Possible remittance basis (refer to diagram)

Personal tax – overseas aspects

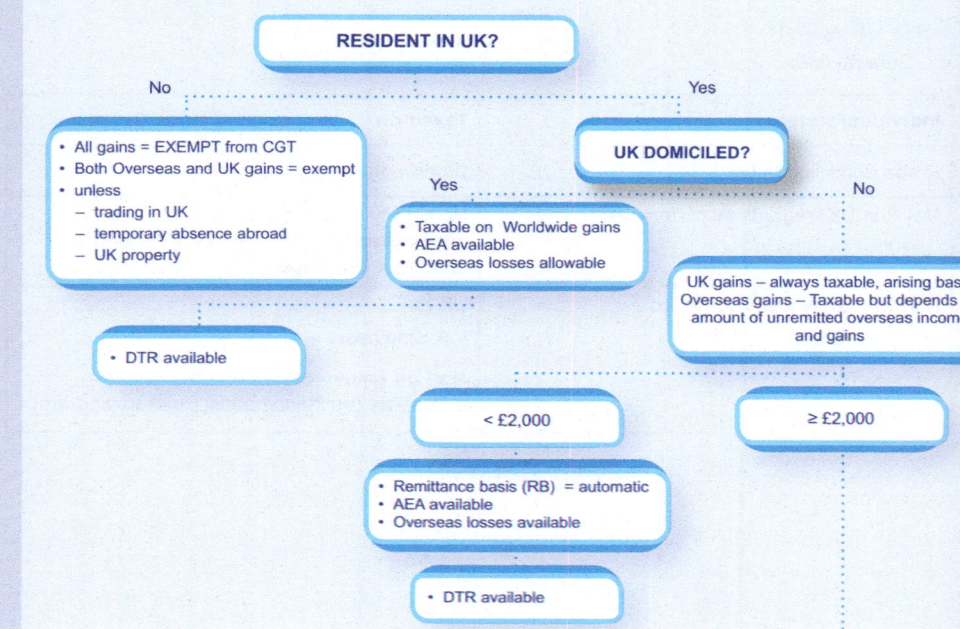

Chapter 14

- Arising basis = automatic
- AEA available
- Overseas losses allowable

BUT

- Can elect for RB (decision made each year)
- One election for both income tax and CGT

If elect:
- No AEA available
- Possible Remittance basis charge (RBC) of £30,000 or £60,000?
  – refer to income tax section

If RB applies – are overseas losses available?
= depends

- DTR available

Make election
- Binding
- Irrevocable
- Overseas losses allowable
  – now and forever
- But subject to complicated matching rules (not examinable)

No election
- Overseas losses not allowable
  – now or ever

Personal tax – overseas aspects

Individual coming to the UK

Key Point

Only taxed on gains made after becoming UK resident, subject to domicile rules for overseas assets.

Individual leaving the UK

Key Point

- If UK resident for 4 of the previous 7 tax years before leaving the UK.
- UK residents remain liable to CGT even though no longer UK resident **if absent from UK for < 5 years.**
- To avoid the rules and for gains to be exempt: (refer to diagram).

Exam focus

Exam kit questions on this area:

Section A questions
- Hahn Ltd Group
- Dilip Group and Emma

Section B questions
- Cate and Ravi
- Max
- Mirtoon

Exam focus

You may be asked to consider the CGT position of an individual coming to the UK and leaving the UK.

Temporary absence abroad

```
┌─────────────────────────────────┐
│  Individual leaving the UK for  │
│  period of temporary absence    │
└─────────────────────────────────┘
                │
                ▼
    ┌──────────────────────┐
    │  Period whilst abroad: │
    │       No CGT           │
    └──────────────────────┘
                │
                ▼
     ┌──────────────────────┐
     │  On re-entry into the UK:  │
     └──────────────────────┘
           /            \
```

Return within five years:
Liable on
- disposals of all assets whilst abroad, if the asset was owned before leaving the UK
- disposals after the date of return

Return after five years:
Liable on
- disposals after the date of return only
- No CGT on disposals whilst abroad (unless UK property)

Non-UK residents and UK property disposals

Non-UK resident individuals are subject to CGT on the disposal of UK property:

- Disposals of UK residential property after 5 April 2015.
- Disposals of UK non-residential property after 5 April 2019.

UK residential property

Only gains arising from 5 April 2015 are subject to CGT.

For exam purposes only properties acquired after 5 April 2015 will be tested so no special rules apply.

PRR for non-UK resident individuals

- PRR available as usual for periods of occupation and deemed occupation (Chapter 6).
- For periods of non-residence, if the individual/spouse/civil partner:
  - stayed in the property for at least 90 nights in the tax year
    = treat **actual occupation** as period of **occupation**
  - did not stay in the property for at least 90 nights in the tax year
    = treat the **whole tax year** as a period of **non-occupation**
    (i.e. ignore actual occupation).

UK non-residential property

Only the gain arising after 5 April 2019 is subject to CGT.

Non-residential property purchased after 5 April 2019:

- calculate gain (or loss) before reliefs in the normal way.

Non-residential property purchased before April 2019:

- use MV at 5 April 2019 as deemed cost (or elect to use actual cost instead).

Exam focus

Exam kit questions on this area:

Section B questions

- Mirtoon
- Pinto

Double tax relief

Double tax relief

Deduct from the individual's capital gains tax liability

Lower of:

- Overseas capital gains tax suffered
- UK capital gains tax on the disposal of that overseas asset

Note:

- The AEA amount and any capital losses are allocated against UK gains first.
- When calculating UK tax on overseas gains, treat as 'top slice'.

Inheritance tax

- General rule:

Individual's status	Taxed on
UK domiciled	Worldwide assets
Not UK domiciled	UK assets only

- Deemed domicile
  - An individual who ceases to be UK domiciled remains deemed UK domiciled for IHT purposes for a further 3 years.
  - An individual who has been resident in the UK for ≥ 15 out of the last 20 tax years and for at least 1 of the last 4 tax years, ending with the tax year in question, is deemed UK domiciled.
  - An individual who was born in the UK, who is UK resident in the tax year and was UK resident for at least 1 of the previous 2 tax years is deemed UK domiciled.

Key Point

Liability to IHT is determined by domicile, not residency.

Chapter 14

Location of assets
(only relevant to non-UK domiciled individuals)

Land and buildings	• Physical location
Registered shares and securities	• Place of registration
Chattels	• Location at time of transfer
Debtors	• Where the debtor resides
Bank accounts	• Location of account
Life assurance policies	• Where proceeds are payable
Interest in a business	• Where the business is carried on

Exam focus

You may be asked to consider the IHT position of an individual coming to the UK and leaving the UK.

Individual leaving the UK

Key Point

- Liable to IHT on worldwide assets
  - for 3 years after leaving UK (deemed UK domiciled).
- If acquire a non-UK domicile of choice:
  - will only be liable on UK assets once 3 years have elapsed.

Personal tax – overseas aspects

Individual coming to the UK

Key Point

- If acquire a UK domicile of choice:
  - liable on worldwide assets when become UK domiciled.
- If remain non-UK domiciled:
  - deemed UK domiciled and liable on worldwide assets when been resident in UK for 15 out of last 20 tax years.

Exam focus

Exam kit questions on this area:

Section A questions

- Heyer Ltd Group
- Olma and Hogan

Double tax relief

Deduct:

- from IHT on estate
- after QSR
- Lower of:
  - overseas death duties
  - UK IHT on overseas asset.

Note:

- UK IHT on overseas asset
  = (Amount included in estate)
  x average rate of IHT after QSR.

chapter 15

Personal tax planning

In this chapter

- Personal tax planning – overview.
- Income tax planning.
- Capital gains tax planning.
- Inheritance tax planning.
- Tax efficient income.
- Tax efficient expenditure.
- Tax efficient remuneration.
- Employment versus self-employment.
- Married couples/civil partners tax planning.
- Lifetime giving versus legacies on death.

Personal tax planning

Exam focus

In the examination you may need to be able to identify and advise on the types of investment and other expenditure that will result in a reduction in income tax liabilities for an individual.

You must also be able to identify the appropriate taxes applicable to a given scenario and advise on suitable tax planning measures to mitigate the personal tax liabilities of an individual.

Personal tax planning – overview

Personal tax planning involves consideration of the:

- income tax
- NIC
- capital gains tax
- inheritance tax, and
- stamp taxes

implications of various courses of action.

Primary aim = usually to maximise the individual's 'net after tax cash flow' position.

Income tax planning

Standard income tax planning measures include:

- investing in tax efficient income
- incurring tax efficient expenditure
- maximising use of allowances and basic rate band
- negotiating tax efficient remuneration
- tax planning for married couples/civil partners.

Capital gains tax planning

Standard capital gains tax planning measures include:

- maximising use of AEA
- paying tax at lowest rate
- effective utilisation of capital losses
- effective use of CGT reliefs
- timing the acquisition and disposal of capital assets
- tax planning for married couples/civil partners.

Inheritance tax planning

Standard inheritance tax planning measures include:

- maximising use of lifetime exemptions (e.g. annual exemption, marriage exemption, small gifts, normal expenditure out of income)
- making lifetime gifts of appreciating assets (but be aware of CGT implications)
- making PETs as soon as possible (exempt if survive seven years)
- effective use of IHT reliefs
- maximising use of the nil rate band
- use of a deed of variation.

Common examination scenarios:

- Recommending tax efficient income and expenditure.
- Considering alternative forms of remuneration
    - Employment versus self-employment.
- Tax planning for married couples/civil partners.
- Lifetime giving versus leaving a legacy in a will.

Exam focus

- Exam kit questions on CGT and IHT planning:

Section A questions

- Ray, Shanira and Kelly

Section B questions

- Liber

Tax efficient income
- Exempt income – Chapter 11.
- Tax exempt benefits – Chapter 12.

Tax efficient expenditure

	Maximum rate of tax relief
• Pension contributions	45%
• Qualifying loan interest	45% on up to greater of £50,000 or 25% of ATI
• Employment expenses	45%
• EIS investment	30% on investment up to £1 million
• SEIS investment	50% on investment up to £200,000
• VCT investment	30% on investment up to £200,000

Tax efficient remuneration

- Maximising use of exempt benefits
  - Chapter 12.
- Considering the provision of company car versus self purchase and mileage allowance or cash alternative (below).
- Receiving tax advantaged versus non-tax advantaged share options – Chapter 12.
- Comparing employment packages
  - Chapter 12.

Exam focus

Exam kit questions on this area:

Section A questions
- Grand Ltd Group

Section B questions
- Hyssop Ltd
- Methley Ltd

Company car versus self-purchase and mileage allowance or cash alternative

Company car	Self purchase and mileage allowance or cash alternative

• Additional income tax liability on:
  – Taxable car benefit
  – Possible fuel benefit.
• No running costs borne by individual employee.
• Employer liable to class 1A NICs.
• Costs of providing car and fuel, including class 1A NICs.
  = allowable deductions against trading profits.
	• If mileage allowance received > AMAP: additional income tax liability and class 1 NICs payable on excess.
	• If mileage allowance received < AMAP: allowable deduction from employment income.
	• Additional income tax and class 1 NICs liability on any cash alternative received.
	• Individual employee bears running costs of car.
	• Employer liable to employer's class 1 NICs on excess mileage allowance and cash alternative.
	• Mileage allowance, or cash alternative, including class 1 NICs
	  = allowable deductions against trading profits.

Employment versus self-employment

- Decision = based on facts.
- No one factor is overriding.
- Consider all of the facts presented and apply the following factors:

Factors to consider	Employed Contract of service	Self-employed Contract for services
Control of work	Employee is directed/instructed on how and when to work by the employer.	Can choose hours, method, location and can sub-contract work to others. Is contracted to produce a result and is not directed in how to achieve that result.
Obligations	Employee has right to expect work and cannot decline the work nor sub-contract the work to others outside the organisation.	Has no right to expect further work once the contract is completed and has no obligation to perform further work.
Risk	No personal financial risk to own capital, not responsible for correction of bad work, paid regardless of whether or not the business is profitable.	Risk financial loss of capital, personally responsible for correction of bad work, risk of no return if loss-making.

Factors to consider	Employed Contract of service	Self-employed Contract for services
Pay	Governed by employment legislation (i.e. regular pay, holiday pay, sick pay) and paid under PAYE system.	No employment rights, paid when work completed and invoice rendered.
Equipment	Employer provides.	Provides own.
Clients	Usually works wholly or mainly for one organisation.	Usually works for many customers.

Personal tax planning

- Employed = taxed according to employment income rules
  - On a receipts basis.
  - Allowable deductions = wholly, exclusively and necessarily incurred.
  - Class 1 NICs payable.
  - Tax collected under PAYE.
- Self-employed = taxed according to trading income rules
  - Allowable deductions = wholly and exclusively incurred.
  - Class 4 NICs payable.
  - Tax collected under self-assessment.
- Advantages of self-employment
  - More allowable expense deductions.
  - Lower total NICs payable.
  - Later payment of income tax and NICs.

Married couples/civil partners tax planning

Income tax

The following income tax planning advice should be given to married couples and couples in a civil partnership:

- Equalise income.
- Maximise use of tax-free investments.
- Maximise pension contributions.
- Maximise use of available allowances.

Exam focus

Exam kit questions on this area:

Section A questions

- Heyer Ltd Group

Equalising income

- Aim = to ensure full use of the couple's PAs, savings NRBs, dividend NRBs and BRBs, and to minimise the amount of tax liable at the higher rate/additional rate.
- Consider ownership of income producing assets (i.e. sole versus joint ownership).
- Make declaration to vary the split of joint income if advantageous.
- Redistribute income producing assets to minimise the couple's liability.

Spouse/civil partner as partner or employee

- Employment income is not transferable but if one of the couple is a sole trader, consider implications of creating a partnership with the spouse/civil partner versus employing the spouse/civil partner.

Partner	Employee
• split income in any proportion, as desired	• income tax relief on gross employment costs
• no tax relief for drawings	• class 1 employee and employer's contributions payable
• class 4 NICs payable	

Capital gains tax

The ability to transfer capital assets between spouses/civil partners with no CGT consequences provides the opportunity to:

- Effectively equalise income (as above) without incurring CGT.
- Ensure both spouses/civil partners use their AEAs each year.
- Ensure gains are realised by the spouse/civil partner who has capital losses.
- Ensure remaining gains are left with the spouse with the lowest income.

Chapter 15

Inheritance tax

- Skip a generation
  (i.e. gift to grandchildren)
  - no immediate IHT saving
  - IHT saved on death of children.
- Enter into deed of variation to increase legacies to:
  - spouse/civil partner, and/or
  - charity to reduce the rate of tax.
- If recipient spouse/civil partner is non-UK domiciled
  - consider election to be treated as UK domiciled.
- Leave qualifying residential property to direct descendants to qualify for residence nil rate band.

Exam focus

Exam kit questions on IHT planning:

Section A questions

- Gail and Brad
- Heyer Ltd Group and Dee

Lifetime giving versus legacies on death

Advantage of lifetime gifts	Disadvantages of lifetime gifts

• Reduces IHT payable on death as assets gifted during lifetime are removed from the chargeable estate.
 	
   Note – no reduction in the value of the chargeable estate if the assets gifted get BPR or APR at 100%.
 	
• IHT on lifetime gifts likely to be less than IHT in death estate because:
   – IHT = £Nil if the donor lives for > 7 years.
   – the value is frozen at the date of the gift, therefore by gifting an appreciating asset during lifetime, the IHT is based on a lower amount.
   – the value subject to IHT is less as lifetime exemptions such AE, ME, small gift relief available.
   – taper relief available if the donor lives for > 3 years.
	• Loss of income and use of the capital if assets given away.
	
	• CGT may be payable if the assets gifted during lifetime are chargeable assets for CGT whereas no CGT if gifted on death.
	
	• APR or BPR on lifetime gift withdrawn if donee does not retain asset at donor death, better to secure BPR/APR by retaining asset in donor's estate.
	
	• RNRB not available on lifetime gift of residential property.

chapter 16

Business tax

In this chapter

- Starting in business.
- Cessation of business.
- Incorporation relief.
- Trading losses.
- Partnerships.
- Self-assessment for the self-employed.

Business tax

Exam focus

For unincorporated businesses (which includes sole traders and partnerships) there is little new technical knowledge at ATX but you must now be able to handle business tax within a multi-tax scenario.

Be prepared to evaluate alternative strategies (e.g. in relation to losses), and to explain your recommendations.

Decision making is also likely to be a key area including 'lease versus buy' decisions and whether it is better from a tax point of view to use employed or self-employed staff in the business.

Exam focus

Exam kit questions on this area:

Section B questions

- Meg and Laurie
- Jessica
- Rod

Starting in business

Key areas to consider for a new business scenario:

1 Income tax

A Badges of trade

= factors used to determine if an activity constitutes:

- trading (s.t. income tax) or:
- an investment (s.t. capital gains tax).

- No single test conclusive.
- Consider (SOFIRM): table overleaf.
- Additional factors (FAST):
  - Finance method
  - Acquisition method
  - Similar Transactions.

Exam focus

You need to be able to assess a given situation and express an opinion on whether it constitutes trading.

Exam kit questions on this area:

Section B questions

- Cate and Ravi
- Tomas and Ines

Test		Consider
Subject matter	S	• Type of good normally traded vs personal asset. • Income producing.
Ownership period	O	• Sale within short period indicates trading.
Frequency of transactions	F	• Repeated similar transactions indicate trading. • Single transaction may however constitute trading (e.g. toilet rolls case).
Improvements	I	• Work carried out to make asset more marketable may indicate trading.
Reason for sale	R	• Forced sale to raise cash indicates not trading.
Motive	M	• Intention to profit from transaction indicates trading. • Absence of profit motive does not prevent being deemed to be trading.

Remember: SOFIRM

B Trading income

Exam focus

You are more likely to be given a tax adjusted trading profits figure in the question than have to calculate it at ATX. However, it is still important to remember the basic principles and computations

Unincorporated businesses (sole traders and partnerships) can calculate tax adjusted trading profits/losses on:

- cash basis (by default), or
- accruals basis (by election).

Exam focus

In the exam you should assume the cash basis applies, unless told otherwise.

Cash basis

- Calculate tax adjusted trading profits for each accounting period as follows:

	£
Trading receipts (including sale of equipment)	X
Less: Allowable expenses paid (including purchase of equipment)	(X)
Tax adjusted trading profits before capital allowances	X
Less: Capital allowances:	
Cars only (unless mileage allowance claimed – later)	(X)
Tax adjusted trading profits after capital allowances	X

Advantages
- Simpler accounting.
- Profit taxed when realised and cash available to pay.

Disadvantage
- Expenses only deductible when paid.

Accruals basis
- If elect.
- Calculate tax adjusted trading profits for each accounting period as follows:

		£
Net profit per accounts		X
Add back:	Non-trading expenses (disallowable expenditure)	X
	Trading income not credited in the accounts	X
Deduct:	Non-trading income	(X)
	Trading expenses not charged in the accounts	(X)
Tax adjusted trading profits before capital allowances		X
Less:	Capital allowances:	
	Plant and machinery (later)	(X)
	Structures and buildings allowance (Chapter 1)	(X)
Tax adjusted trading profits after capital allowances		X

Summary of differences between cash basis and accruals basis

	Cash basis	Accruals basis
Method of calculation	• Usually start with trade receipts and deduct allowable expenditure	• Usually start with net profit per accounts and adjust for non-trade and disallowable items included in net profit
Revenue and expenses	• Include revenue **received** and expenses **paid** in accounting period	• Include revenue **earned** and expenses **incurred** in accounting period (i.e. follow accounts)
Capital expenditure: Plant and machinery	• Deduct cost (except cars) • Add proceeds on sale (except cars) • Capital allowances available on cars only	• No deduction for cost • Add back depreciation • Add back loss on disposal • Deduct profit on disposal • Capital allowances available
Capital expenditure: Land and buildings	• No deduction for cost • No SBAs	• No deduction for cost • Add back depreciation • SBAs may be available (Chapter 2)

	Cash basis	Accruals basis
Short lease premiums (< 50 years)	• No deduction for premium paid	• Add back amortisation • Deduct property income taxed on landlord (Chapter 11) spread over life of lease
Hired and leased cars	• No restriction for high emissions • Deduct business proportion of cost	• Disallow 15% of lease costs if CO_2 emissions > 50g/km • Further adjustment for private use of owner
Goods for own use	• Not examinable	• Add back selling price (if not adjusted in accounts) • Add back profit (if adjusted in accounts)

Flat rate expenses

Any unincorporated business (whether they are using the cash basis or the accruals basis) can:

- opt to use flat rate expense adjustments
- to replace the calculation of actual costs incurred in respect of certain expenses.

Type of expense	Flat rate expense adjustment
Motoring expenses = capital or lease costs, and running costs (e.g. insurance, repairs, servicing and fuel)	Allowable deduction = amount using the AMAP rates of 45p and 25p per mile (Note 1) For purchased cars, this is instead of deducting capital allowances and running costs
Private use of part of a commercial building (e.g. guest house)	Adjustment = fixed amount based on the number of occupants (Note 2). Covers: private use of household goods and services, food and utilities

Notes: If required:

1. AMAP rates are given in tax rates and allowances.
2. Fixed amount will be provided within the exam question.
   Private element of other expenses (e.g. rent and rates) = adjusted for as normal.

Business tax

Capital allowances

Exam focus

You may have to advise on the capital allowances available to a business. A reminder of the pro forma is set out overleaf.

Pro forma: Capital allowances computation

	£	Main pool £	Special rate pool £	Short life asset £	Private use asset £	Allowances £
TWDV b/f		X	X	X		
Additions not qualifying for AIA or FYA:						
Second-hand zero-emission cars		X				
Cars (1 – 50g/km)		X				
Cars (over 50g/km)			X			
Car with private use					X	
Additions qualifying for AIA:						
Special rate pool expenditure	X					
AIA (Max £1,000,000 in total)	(X)					X
Transfer balance to special rate pool			X			
Plant and machinery	X					
AIA (Max £1,000,000 in total)	(X)					X
Transfer balance to main pool		X				
Disposals (lower of original cost or sale proceeds)		(X)		(X)		
		X	X	X	X	X

Business tax

	£	Main pool £	Special rate pool £	Short life asset £	Private use asset £	Allowance £
BA / (BC)				X / (X)		X / (X)
Small pools WDA						
WDA @ 18%		(X)				X
WDA @ 6%			(X)			X
WDA @ 6%/18% (depending on emissions)					(X) × BU%	X
Additions qualifying for FYAs:						
New zero-emission cars	X					
FYA at 100%	(X)					X
	0					
TWDV c/f		X	X		X	
Total allowances						X

The Annual Investment Allowance (AIA)

- Available to all businesses.
- 100% allowance for the first £1,000,000 of expenditure incurred in each accounting period of 12 months.
- Applied pro rata for periods of account that are not 12 months.
- Available on acquisitions in the order:
    - special rate pool items
    - plant and machinery in main pool
    - short life assets
    - private use assets.
- **Not** available on cars.
- Not available in the accounting period in which trade ceases.
- Expenditure above the maximum qualifies for WDA immediately.
- Taxpayer does not have to claim all / any of the AIA if this is preferable.
- Any unused AIA is lost.
- The AIA must be split between related businesses.

    Businesses owned by the same individual are related where:
    - they are engaged in the same activities, or
    - share the same premises.

    In such circumstances the owner of the businesses can choose how to allocate a single AIA between them.

- Unrelated businesses owned by the same individual will each be entitled to the full AIA.

Business tax

Writing down allowance (WDA)

- Available to all businesses.
- WDA available on a reducing balance basis.
- 18% on main pool and on SLAs.
- Special rate pool WDA = 6%.
- Applied pro rata for periods of account that are not 12 months.
- WDA adjusted for assets with private use by owner of business.

First year allowances (FYA)

- Available to all businesses.
- 100% FYA available on:
  - new zero-emission cars (not available on any other cars)
- Only available in the period of acquisition.
- Never time apportion for short or long accounting periods.
- Taxpayer does not have to claim all/any of the FYA if this is preferable.
- If any of the FYA is not claimed the balance is put in the main pool:
  - but not entitled to WDA until the following period.

Balancing adjustments

- Assets disposed of:
  - Deduct the sale proceeds from the relevant pool.
  - The amount deducted can never exceed the original cost of the asset.
  - A balancing adjustment may arise.

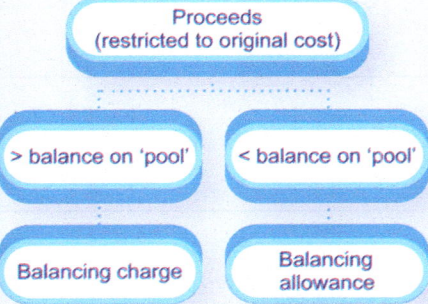

- A balancing charge (BC)
  - Can occur in any pool at any time.
- A balancing allowance (BA)
  - Can occur in a 'single asset' column at any time.
  - Only occurs on main pool or special rate when the business ceases to trade.

Summary of the capital allowances available for cars

CO_2 emissions

• Zero-emission:
    – New = FYA 100%
    – Second-hand = as for standard emission cars

• Standard emission:
    – Emissions 1 – 50g/km
    – Put in main pool
    – WDA 18% for a 12-month period

• High emission:
    – Emissions > 50g/km
    – Put in special rate pool
    – WDA 6% for a 12-month period

• Private use cars
    – Separate column
    – WDA 18%/6% for 12-month period depending on emissions
    – BA or BC will arise on disposal

The special rate pool

- Pools expenditure incurred on:
  - long-life assets (LLA)
  - integral features of a building
  - thermal insulation of a building
  - high emission cars (CO_2 > 50g/km).
- Pool operates in the same way as the main pool.
- AIA is available on new expenditure in this pool first (except high emission cars).
- WDA = 6% for a 12-month period, reducing balance basis.
- FYA is never available.
- LLA = assets
  - with a working life ≥ 25 years, and
  - expenditure incurred ≥ £100,000 for a 12-month period (but not cars or P&M in a retail shop, showroom, hotel or office).

- Integral features
  = expenditure incurred on:
  - electrical (including lighting) systems
  - cold water systems
  - space or water heating systems
  - external solar shading
  - powered systems of ventilation, air cooling or air purification
  - lifts, escalators and moving walkways.
- Thermal insulation of a building
  = expenditure on thermal insulation on any commercial building (other than residential buildings in a property business).

Exam focus

Exam kit questions on this area:
Section A questions
- Jake

The small pool WDA

- Applies to the main pool and special rate pool only
  - can claim on either or both pools
  - claim is optional.
- Available where the balance on the pool after current period additions and disposals is ≤ £1,000.
- WDA = any amount up to £1,000 for a 12-month period.
- Applied pro rata if period of account is not 12 months.

Short life assets (SLA)

- Each short life asset has its own column
- Short life means < 9 years useful life.
- AIA available.
- A balancing allowance or charge will arise when the asset is disposed of.
- Beneficial where the asset with a short life is to be disposed of at less than TWDV.
- Not available on cars.
- If asset not disposed of within 8 years from the end of the accounting period in which it was acquired
  - the TWDV is transferred back into the main pool.
- Election required for SLA treatment:
  - by first anniversary of 31 January following the end of the tax year in which the trading period, in which the asset was acquired, ends.

Private use assets
(Unincorporated businesses only)

- Separate column for each private use asset.
- Pool is:
  - written down by the AIA/WDA in full, according to the length of the accounting period, or FYA
  - but actual allowance claimed is restricted to business use proportion.
- BC/BA on disposal are also restricted to business use proportion.
- Cannot claim SLA treatment.
- Not applicable for companies.

Exam focus

Exam kit questions with plant and machinery allowances:

Section A questions

- Ziti
- Plad Ltd and Quil Ltd
- Pippin
- Jake

Approach to computational questions

For P&M capital allowances, adopt the following step-by-step approach:

(1) Read the information in the question and decide how many columns / pools you will require.

(2) Draft the layout and insert the TWDV b/f (does not apply in a new trade).

(3) Insert additions not eligible for the AIA or FYAs into the appropriate column taking particular care to allocate cars into the correct column according to CO_2 emissions.

(4) Insert additions eligible for the AIA in the first column, then allocate the AIA to the additions.

Remember to time apportion if period of account is not 12 months.

Allocate the AIA to special rate pool additions in priority to additions of P&M in the main or individual asset pools.

(5) Any special rate pool additions in excess of the AIA must be added to the special rate pool column to increase the balance available for 6% WDA.

Any main pool expenditure, in excess of the AIA, should be added to the main pool to increase the balance qualifying for 18% WDA.

(6) Deal with any disposal by deducting the lower of cost or sale proceeds.

(7) Work out any balancing charge / balancing allowance for single asset columns.

Remember to adjust for any private use if an unincorporated business (not relevant for companies).

(8) Consider if the small pools WDA applies to the main pool and / or the special rate pool.

(9) Calculate the WDA on each of the pools at the appropriate rate (18% or 6%).

Remember to:
- time apportion if the period of account is not 12 months
- adjust for any private use if an unincorporated business (not relevant for companies).

(10) Insert any additions of new zero-emission cars eligible for 100% FYA.

Remember the FYA is never time apportioned.

(11) Calculate the TWDV to carry forward to the next accounting period and add the allowances column.

(12) Deduct the total allowances from the tax adjusted trading profits.

Structures and buildings allowances (SBAs)

Available as for companies (Chapter 1):
- commercial (not residential) property
- 3% on qualifying cost
- from the date the building comes into use.

SBAs must be scaled up or down according to the length of accounting period
- could be > 12 months for an unincorporated business.

Basis of assessment

Exam focus

You must know how adjusted trading profits are assessed to income tax.
- For tax years up to 2022/23:
  - **Current year basis**
    = 12-month accounting period ending in the tax year.
  - Special rules for opening and closing years (not examinable).

- Tax year 2023/24:
  - **Transitional year** = any profits not yet taxed less overlap relief.

Transition profits
  - May arise in 2023/24.
  - Spread over five years (default), or
  - can **elect** to tax earlier.
  - Separate entry in income tax computation.

Exam focus

The amount of transition profits arising in 2023/24 and any amounts already taxed will be provided.

- Tax year 2024/25 onwards:
  - **Tax year basis** = profits **arising** in the tax year.
  - If business does not have 31 March/5 April year end = profits must be **time apportioned** into the tax year.
  - If business **starts** during 2024/25 = profits from date of commencement to 5 April 2025.

VAT
- Compulsory registration.
- Voluntary registration.

Refer to Chapter 18.

Exam focus

You may be required to determine when a business should register for VAT, identify advantages and disadvantages of registering earlier and penalties for late registration.

National insurance contributions (NIC)

- A sole trader has NIC liabilities based on the business profits together with additional NIC liabilities if the business employs staff.

Self-employed

Class 4
- Paid on taxable trade profits less losses b/f.
- Rate of 6% of profits which fall between £12,570 and £50,270.
- Rate of 2% on profits which exceed £50,270.
- Paid at the same time as income tax under self-assessment.
- Not payable if over state pension age or under 16 at the **start** of the tax year.

Key Point

Self-employed individuals who have employees pay:

- class 4 NICs in respect of their unincorporated trade, and
- employer's class 1 and class 1A NICs in respect of earnings and benefits provided to employees.

Exam focus

Exam kit questions with NIC aspects:

Section A questions
- Pippin
- Mita and Snowdon
- Ray, Shanira and Kelly

Section B questions
- Tomas and Ines

Business tax

Cessation of business

Exam focus

This scenario may be examined in the following circumstances:

- Sole trader sells the business to another sole trader.
- Sole trader sells the business to a company (incorporation of a business).
- Sole trader gifts the business.
- A partner leaves the partnership.
- Sole trader retires or dies.

Exam kit questions on this area:

Section A questions

- Ziti
- Waverley and Set Ltd Group

Section B questions

- Mirtoon
- Sabin and Patan Ltd

Consider the following taxes for each of the scenarios:

1. **Income tax**
   - Capital allowances:
     - Additions and disposals are allocated to relevant pools
     - No AIA/FYA/WDA given in final period
     - Compute balancing allowances (BA) or charges (BC)
     - If business transferred to connected person (i.e. business incorporated)
       - can elect to transfer at TWDV (no BAs or BCs).
   - Plant and machinery under cash basis
     - Include disposal proceeds as trading receipt (except cars)
     - No adjustment for car disposals, no capital allowances claimed.

- Trading income assessment
  - Final tax year = tax year in which trade ceases:
    - tax profits from 6 April to cessation
    - include remaining transition profits.
- Post-cessation income
  - Taxed in **tax year of receipt** as miscellaneous income, or
  - Claim to tax in tax year of cessation (if received in 6 tax years following cessation).
  - Claim by 31 January 2027 for receipts in 2024/25.
- Post-cessation expenses
  - Offset against post-cessation income in tax year expense is paid.
  - Only relievable if paid < 7 years of cessation of trade.
  - Claim relief by 31 January 2027 for deductions in 2024/25.

2 Capital gains tax

- Chargeable gains arise on disposal of assets (e.g. goodwill, property, investments).
- MV used as proceeds if assets gifted.
- Consider available reliefs:

Sale of business	BADR
	EIS/SEIS reinvestment relief
	Incorporation relief if sold to a company (later in this chapter)
	Rollover relief
Sale to company in exchange for shares	Incorporation relief (later in this chapter)
Gift of business	Gift holdover relief

3 Inheritance tax

- Consider availability of business property relief on gift of an unincorporated business (Chapter 8).

4 VAT

- Deregister when cease to make taxable supplies.

Situation	VAT position
Individual assets sold	Normal VAT rules apply (Chapter 18)
Assets held at date of cessation of trade	Deemed supply of business assets e.g. P&M, inventory, at MV at date of cessation (De minimis limit £1,000)
Business transferred as going concern, and • Assets used in same kind of business as transferor, and • Transferee is or immediately becomes registered for VAT.	No VAT – not a taxable supply

Chapter 16

Exam focus

Exam kit questions on this area:

Section A questions
- Ziti

Section B questions
- Enid
- Mirtoon

Business tax

Incorporation relief

- Where an individual incorporates a sole trade or partnership business:
  - chargeable gains arise on the MV of the individual assets transferred.
- Incorporation relief is a relief which
  - automatically applies
  - to defer the net chargeable gains arising on incorporation
  - provided certain conditions are met.

Exam focus

Exam kit questions on this area:
Section A questions

- Waverley and Set Ltd Group
- Hiromi
- Mita and Snowdon

Section B questions

- Enid

Key Point

Where consideration is wholly shares:
- No gain on incorporation.
- Gains deferred until the subsequent disposal of shares.

Where non-share consideration is received:
- a chargeable gain arises on incorporation
- taxed at 0%, 10%, or 20% depending on the availability of the AEA, BADR and level of taxable income.

Conditions	• All of the assets of the business (except cash) must be transferred.
	• The transfer must be of a business as a going concern.
	• The consideration received must be wholly or partly in shares.
Effect	• No gains arise on incorporation.
	• Gains are deferred against the acquisition cost of the shares.
Consideration not wholly in shares	• Gain eligible for deferral: $$\text{Gain} \times \frac{\text{Value of shares issued}}{\text{Total consideration}}$$
	• Immediate gain in respect of non-share consideration which is taxed at 10% or 20%: $$\text{Gain} \times \frac{\text{Value of non-shares consideration}}{\text{Total consideration}}$$
Future disposal of shares	• On a later sale of the shares, the gain will normally qualify for BADR provided conditions satisfied.
	• Where shares are received on incorporation the pre-transfer ownership period can be taken into consideration when deciding if the 2 year condition is satisfied.

| Election to disapply | - Can elect for incorporation relief not to apply.
| | - Gains on the assets transferred to the company would be taxed at 0%, 10%, or 20% depending on the availability of the AEA, BADR and level of taxable income.
| | - No gains would be deferred against the cost of the shares, making the gain on their subsequent disposal lower.
| | - May be beneficial to elect to disapply if:
| | – gains covered by AEA, or
| | – shares would not be eligible for BADR as individual doesn't own 5% of the company or isn't an employee of the company.
| | - Must elect within 2 years from 31 January following the end of the tax year in which the business is transferred.
| | - For 2024/25 by 31 January 2028.

Planning points

- Must transfer all assets
  - may wish to retain property with large growth potential to avoid double charge to tax
  - consider gift holdover relief as an alternative to transfer selected assets
  - as goodwill transferred to a related close company is not eligible for BADR, it could be efficient to defer the gains under incorporation relief. When the gain becomes chargeable on disposal of the shares, BADR can be claimed provided the share disposal qualifies.
- Defers gains pre BADR
  - consider electing to disapply incorporation relief if unlikely to hold 5% of the company or be an employee of the company.

Exam focus

Questions involving incorporation may require detailed knowledge of incorporation relief, gift holdover relief and BADR.

Trading losses

Be prepared to apply your knowledge to a particular scenario, compare alternative strategies and explain your recommendations.

Trading losses
- Calculated in the same way as a trading profit.
- Trading income assessment is £Nil.

Relief against total income
- Available in:
  - tax year of the loss and/or,
  - preceding tax year.

- Offset can not be restricted to preserve PA.
- Offset is restricted if loss exceeds maximum amount (later in chapter).
- Excess loss is automatically carried forward or can be set against chargeable gains.

Relief against chargeable gains
- Available in the same years as a claim against total income:
  - tax year of the loss, and/or
  - preceding tax year.
- Only possible after a claim against total income has been made in the tax year in which a claim against gains is required.
- Do not need to claim against total income in both years first.
- No maximum restriction.

Relief against future trading profits

- Relieved against:
  - the first available
  - trading profits only
  - of the same trade.
- Loss offset cannot be restricted.

- Trading loss is treated as a current year capital loss
- Deducted
  - after the offset of current year capital losses
  - before the AEA, and
  - before capital losses brought forward.

Order of offset

When there is more than one loss to offset:

- deal with the earliest loss first
- losses b/f are offset in priority to CY and PY claims
- watch out for the maximum restriction (if applicable) (later in chapter).

Reduced capital allowances claim

- Loss arising can be reduced by **not** claiming full capital allowances.
- The TWDV c/f for CAs will be correspondingly higher.
- Higher CAs will therefore be claimed in the future rather than creating or increasing a loss now.

Opening years relief

In addition to reliefs available for an ongoing business, special opening year loss relief is available.

- A loss incurred in any of the **first four tax years** of a new business can be set against:
    - total income
    - of the three tax years preceding the year of the loss
    - on a FIFO basis.
- One claim covers all three years.
- Offset cannot be restricted to preserve PA.
- Maximum restriction applies as for ongoing loss relief against total income.

Business tax

Terminal loss relief

In addition to standard relief against total income and chargeable gains, special terminal loss relief is available.

Relief is given for the loss of the **final 12 months** of trading.

- Relief is:
  - against profits of the same trade
  - of the tax year of cessation, and
  - the three preceding tax years
  - on a LIFO basis.

Business transferred to company

- Business transferred to company.
- In exchange wholly/mainly for shares (80% of consideration).
- Trading losses at date of cessation carried forward indefinitely provided owner retains shares.
- Offset against future income received from company **in any order**:
  - earned income (salary, bonus)
  - interest
  - dividends.

Maximum deduction from total income

Maximum deduction from income other than trading income = **greater of**:

- £50,000, or
- 25% of adjusted total income (ATI).

Therefore restriction will be £50,000 unless ATI exceeds £200,000.

Adjusted total income (ATI):

	£
Total income	X
Less: Gross PPCs	(X)
ATI	X

Key Point

The maximum restriction may be beneficial as it could avoid wasting PAs.

Maximum deduction limit:

- applies to trading losses set against:
  - current year total income
  - earlier years **if** set against income other than profits of the same trade.
- does not apply to losses set against chargeable gains.

Offset against earlier years:

- set against profits from same trade first, then non-trading income
- no restriction to offset against profits from same trade
- restrict offset against non-trading income
- loss that cannot be set off = not lost
  - can claim to offset against chargeable gains, or
  - c/f as usual.

Business tax

Procedure for dealing with questions involving losses

(1) Determine tax adjusted loss/profits after capital allowances for each tax year.

(2) Lay out IT computations for tax years side by side.
   - Leave spaces to insert losses offset.

(3) Set up a loss working for each loss to show how it is utilised.

(4) If more than one loss.
   - Consider in chronological order.

(5) Consider options available depending on whether early year, last year, chargeable gains in tax year.

(6) Offset losses in most beneficial way:
   - Obtaining relief at highest rates of tax.
   - Taking relief as soon as possible.
   - Not wasting personal allowances.

   Watch out for the maximum deduction rules.

Exam focus

Exam kit questions on this area:

Section A questions
- Olma and Hogan
- Jonny
- Hiromi

Section B questions
- Sabin and Patan Ltd
- Jessica
- Rosa

Choice of loss reliefs

- Objectives in choosing the most appropriate loss claim:
  - obtain relief at the highest marginal tax rate
  - obtain relief as early as possible
  - avoid wasting PAs (and the AEA for CGT where appropriate).
- Relief against total income and the opening year relief give earliest relief, rather than carrying the loss forward.
- A large gain in a single year (the year of loss or year immediately preceding):
  - indicates a claim against chargeable gains may be beneficial
  - but must relieve total income of same year first and maximum restriction may apply
  - may result in wastage of PAs
  - maximum restriction does not apply against gains
  - relief against gains is at 10% or 20%. (18% or 24% for gains on residential properties).
- Relief against total income and the opening year relief are optional reliefs but carry forward relief is mandatory and automatic if no specific claim is made.
- No partial claims allowed (i.e. all or nothing reliefs).
- Losses can be restricted by making reduced capital allowance claims.
- Relief against total income applies to two years but separate claims are required for each year and such claims can be made in either order.
- The best claim may be a compromise of the main objectives (e.g. may accept lower tax saving if relief is given earlier).

Partnerships

Treat like sole traders – each partner is an owner of the business.

Step 1	Determine the tax adjusted accounting profit/loss after capital allowances of the partnership for each accounting period.
Step 2	Allocate these profits or losses between the partners according to the **profit sharing agreement** (PSA) in the **accounting period**. If PSA requires a salary or interest on capital allocation: • treat as a share of trading profits. The balance of profits or losses: • shared in the profit sharing ratio (PSR). **If a partner joins or leaves during the accounting period:** • treat as if a change in PSR • time apportion profits, apply appropriate PSA to each part.
Step 3	Determine the taxable profit or available loss for the tax year for each partner using the partner's share of the accounting profit/loss. **Partner joins** – standard loss relief options plus opening year loss relief available **Partner leaves** – standard loss relief options plus terminal loss relief available **Other partners** – standard loss relief options only

Exam focus

Exam kit questions on this area:

Section B questions

- Rod
- Rosa
- Jessica

Self-assessment for the self-employed

Tax Year	Due Date for paying the tax	Consequences of paying tax late
First year	• Income tax and class 4 NICs = due on the 31 January following the tax year • If 2024/25 = first tax year of trading, due by 31 January 2026 • Filing date = same date	• Late payment interest at 7.75% for each day payment is late • Additional penalty of at least £100 is levied for late filing of return (Chapter 10)
Second year and thereafter	• Income tax and class 4 NICs = payable in three instalments • If 2024/25 = second or subsequent year: Payment on account 1: – due 31 January 2025 (i.e. 31 January in tax year) Payment on account 2: – due 31 July 2025 (i.e. 31 July following tax year) Balancing payment: – due 31 January 2026 (i.e. 31 January following tax year)	• Late payment interest at 7.75% for each day payment is late • Additional penalty of at least £100 is levied for late filing of return • If the balancing payment is late: – as above, plus extra penalties of at least 5% of the amount due will apply (Chapter 10)

chapter 17

Business finance and tax planning for companies

In this chapter

- Long term finance.
- Short term finance.
- Financing non-current assets.
- Business vehicle.
- Extracting profits from a business.
- Incorporation of a business.
- Close companies.
- Personal service company.
- Withdrawing investment.
- Tax planning for companies.

Long term finance

Debt versus Equity

	Equity	Debt
Maximum amount	• Specified in Articles of Association	• No limit
Return on investment	• Dividends • Only paid if profitable	• Interest • Paid regardless of profitability
Corporate investors	• Dividends received = exempt	• Interest received = taxable
Individual investors	• Basic rate and higher rate taxpayers have savings nil rate bands available • All taxpayers have a £500 dividend nil rate band. Amounts in excess of this will be taxed at 8.75%/33.75%/39.35% depending on the taxpayer's level of income	

Other points	• If not listed:
	   – difficult to issue new shares
	• Owner managed businesses:
	   – may not like control to be diluted
	   – usually issue shares to existing shareholders or family members
		• lender may require security (i.e. a charge over company assets)

Incentives to issue shares

For individuals:
- SEIS relief.
- EIS relief.
- VCT relief.

For companies:
- Substantial shareholding exemption.

Short term finance

- Bank overdraft.
- Short term loans.
- Trade credit.
- Invoice discounting.
- Debt factoring.
- Hire purchase and leasing.

Financing non-current assets

	Outright purchase	Hire purchase	Leasing
Initial outlay	• Full cost	• Instalment	• Lease rental
Subsequent cost of purchase	• None	• Instalments spread over length of HP agreement • Includes HP interest	• Lease rentals spread over length of lease • Includes finance charge
Tax relief against profit	• Capital allowances available	• Interest = allowable deduction against profit • Capital allowances available	• Lease rental = allowable deduction against profit (other than high emission cars with CO_2 > 50g/km where 15% of lease charge is disallowed under the accruals basis) • No capital allowances
VAT recoverable? (except cars)	Yes	Yes	Yes
Sale proceeds on disposal	Yes	Yes	No

Business vehicle

Sole trader versus company

	Sole trader	Company
Taxation of profits	• Tax year basis • Income tax at 20%, 40% or 45% • Based on taxable trading profits • Cash basis or elect for accruals basis • Adjustments for private use • Personal allowance may be available • Class 4 NICs	• Accounting period basis • Corporation tax 19-25% • Based on taxable total profits • Accruals basis • Taxable total profits = after individual's employment income deducted • No adjustments for private use • No personal allowance • No NICs on business profits • Individual pays income tax and class 1 NICs on employment income

	Sole trader (contd)	Company (contd)
Relief for losses	• Available against personal income of individual • Against total income of current and/or previous tax year • Extension claim against chargeable gains in same years • Opening year relief against total income of previous 3 tax years, FIFO basis • Carry forward relief against trading profits of same trade	• Available against company profits only • Against total profits (income and gains) of current year • Carry back 12 months • Carry forward against total profits

Withdrawal of funds	• No tax implications	• Salary/bonus versus dividend (later in chapter)
		• Alternatives:
		  – Rent (but could affect eligibility to BADR)
		  – Pension contributions

VAT	• Individual registers	• Company registers

	Sole trader (contd)	**Company (contd)**

Disposal of business interest	• Disposal of unincorporated business = gains on individual chargeable assets
	• BADR for CGT
	• If gifted:
	   – Gift holdover relief available for CGT
	   – BPR available for IHT
	• If incorporated:
	   – Incorporation relief, or
	   – Gift holdover relief for CGT
		• Disposal of shares
		• BADR
		• If gifted:
		   – Gift holdover relief for CGT may be available
		   – BPR for IHT may be available

Key Point

Where initial losses are anticipated, order events to ensure losses can be relieved against the individual's income and then incorporate business when it becomes profitable.

Extracting profits from a business

	Additional salary (i.e. bonus)	Dividend
Rates of income tax	IT liability = 20%, 40% or 45%	IT liability = 8.75%, 33.75% or 39.35% of dividend
NICs paid by individual	Employee class 1 at 8% or 2%	No NICs payable
NICs paid by company	Employer's class 1 at 13.8%	No NICs payable
Corporation tax implications	Salary and Employer's class 1 NICs = allowable deductions for corporation tax	None
Pension contributions	Salary = relevant earnings for pension relief purposes	Dividends = not relevant earnings for pension relief purposes

Exam focus

Exam kit questions on this area:

Section A questions
- Gail and Brad
- Hiromi

Section B questions
- Traiste Ltd
- Samphire Ltd and Kelp Ltd

Disposal of interest in an unincorporated business

	Income tax	CGT	IHT
Sale of business	- Last adjustment of profits - Last capital allowances - BCs and BAs	- Gains arise on every single chargeable asset - ROR - BADR	- No diminution in value - No IHT
Lifetime gift of business	As above	- Gains arise on every single chargeable asset - Gift holdover relief - BADR	- PET or CLT - BPR = 100% Also available on death provided donee still owns business when donor dies
Death owning business	As above	- No CGT on death	- Business included in Death estate - BPR = 100%

Incorporation of a business

Exam focus

Incorporation is a popular area for examination questions as it can test knowledge of all taxes in the syllabus:

- Income tax
- Corporation tax
- National insurance
- VAT
- SDLT
- Inheritance tax
- Capital gains tax

Exam focus

Exam kit questions on this area:

Section A questions

- Waverley and Set Ltd Group

Section B questions

- Enid

Chapter 17

Incorporation

Income tax
- Formerly profits of trade subject to income tax
- Drawings and private use = not allowable deductions against profit
- Balancing adjustments for CAs (except SBAs) unless succession election applies, or MV as trading receipt under cash basis
- If loss-making incorporation relief available (Chapter 16)

NICs
- Formerly liable to class 4 NICs
- Now liable to employee class 1
- Company liable to employer's class 1 and class 1 A NICs

Value Added Tax
Not a taxable supply
Provided conditions satisfied
(Chapter 18)

Corporation tax
- Profits of trade now subject to corporation tax
- Individual becomes director/shareholder
- Individual taxed on employment income and dividends
- Employment income and employer's NICs = allowable deductions against profit

Capital gains tax
- Disposal of individual assets
- Incorporation relief (Chapter 16) or gift holdover relief available (Chapter 6)

Inheritance tax
- No transfer of value
- No diminution in value

Stamp duty land tax
Payable by the company on purchase of land and buildings

Close companies

Close company = a company with close proprietorial control

(i.e. controlled by five or fewer shareholders or any number of directors usually a family company, an owner managed business)

1 Benefits provided to shareholders

Shareholder	Close company
If shareholder = not an employee • Individual = treated as receiving a dividend. • Subject to income tax at 8.75%, 33.75% or 39.35%. • Value of the deemed cash dividend = the benefit which would have been taxable if they had been an employee of the company.	• Company = treated as paying a dividend to the shareholder. • Costs of providing benefit = not allowable for the company. • No class 1A NICs on deemed dividend.
If shareholder = an employee • Individual = treated as receiving a normal benefit of employment.	• Company = treated as giving a normal benefit to an employee. • Costs of providing benefit = allowable for the company. • Class 1A NICs payable.

2 Loans provided to shareholders

Shareholder	Close company

• If loan is granted with a beneficial rate of interest, the loan benefit assessed as a beneficial loan (refer to benefits above).
• If the loan is written off by the company, the individual
  = treated as receiving a cash dividend equivalent to the loan written off.
• Subject to income tax at 8.75%, 33.75% or 39.35%.
• If shareholder is employee, then write off also subject to class 1 NIC.
	• Company must pay tax charge
	  = 33.75% × loan advance if still outstanding at the normal due date (i.e. 9 months and 1 day after end of the accounting period).
	• Tax charge = payable with corporation tax.
	• Repaid 9 months and 1 day after AP end in which
	  – loan repaid
	  – loan written off.
	• Tax charge does not apply if
	  1 Amount loaned ≤ £15,000, and
	  2 Individual = full time employee, and
	  3 Individual (with associates) owns < 5% interest in the company.

3 Close investment company (CIC)
- Not qualifying interest i.e. not deductible.

4 Shareholder borrows money to buy shares in a close company
- Qualifying loan interest paid
  = allowable relief in shareholder's income tax computation
- reduces taxable income of individual.

Exam focus

Exam kit questions with close company aspects:

Section A questions
- Drench, Paprikash, Hail Ltd and Rain Ltd

Section B questions
- Nocturne Ltd
- Methley Ltd
- Samphire Ltd and Kelp Ltd
- Tula

Personal service company

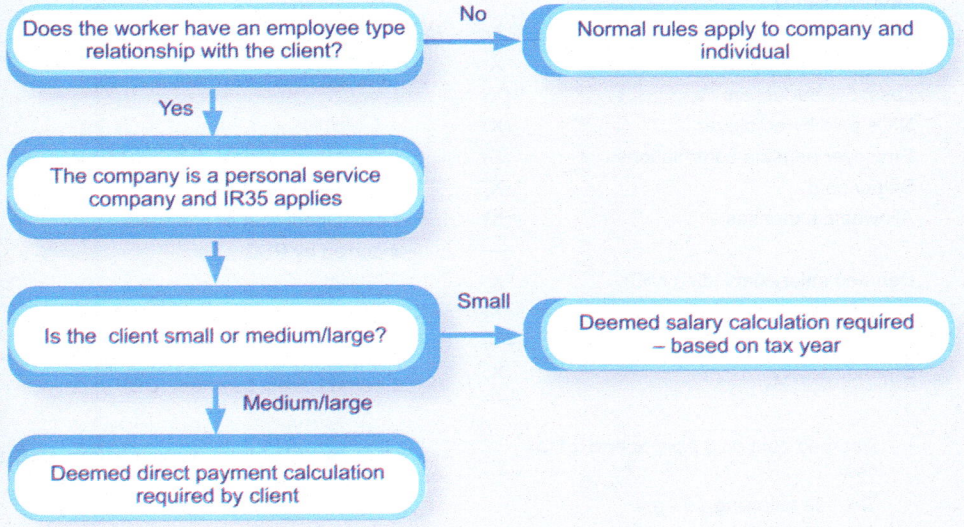

Business finance and tax planning for companies

Small client organisation

Personal service company calculates deemed salary:

	£
Received in tax year	X
Less: 5% deduction	(X)
NICs paid by employer	(X)
Employer pension contributions	(X)
Salary paid	(X)
Allowable expenses	(X)
Deemed salary (including NIC)	X
Less: Employer's NIC	(X)
Deemed salary	X

- Deemed paid on 5 April at end of tax year
- Tax due following 19 April

Medium/large client organisation

Client determines status of worker and issues a Status Determination Statement.

If client decides rules apply it must calculate deemed direct payment:

	£
Payment in respect of services provided (net of VAT)	X
Less: Direct cost of materials incurred by PSC	(X)
Less: Deductible employee expenses incurred by the PSC	(X)
Deemed direct payment (DDP)	X

DDP deducted from payments from PSC to worker before IT and NICs calculated.

Exam focus

Exam kit questions on this area:

Section B questions

- Eric
- Caden and Amahle

Withdrawing investment

Withdrawing investment from a company

Sale of shares

- CGT – payable
- May be difficult to achieve as no ready market for unquoted shares

Purchase of own shares

- Conditions satisfied:
  – capital disposal liable to CGT and BADR if personal trading company
- Conditions not satisfied:
  – treated as dividend = amount received less nominal value of shares

Liquidation of company

- Payments before liquidator appointed = income
- Payments after liquidator appointed = capital
- HMRC allows winding-up without a liquidator and payments to be treated as capital (max £25,000)

Purchase of own shares

Conditions for capital treatment:

(1) The company must be an unquoted trading company.

(2) Be able to demonstrate that the repurchase of the shares is for the benefit of the trade and not part of a scheme to avoid tax.

Examples of benefit to trade:
- buying out retiring directors
- buying out dissident shareholders
- shareholder has died and beneficiaries don't want shares
- venture capitalist withdrawing investment.

(3) The individual must be resident in the UK.

(4) Have owned the shares for 5 years prior to the repurchase (3 years if inherited).

(5) Reduce the shareholding substantially after the buyback – the shareholder must end up with:
- No more than 30% of the shares in the company, and
- No more than 75% of the previous percentage holding.

Exam focus

Exam kit questions with purchase of own shares:

Section A questions
- Olma and Hogan

Section B questions
- Trifles Ltd
- Traiste Ltd
- Maria and Granada Ltd

Exam kit questions with liquidation:

Section A questions
- Joe and Fiona

Section B questions
- Acryl Ltd and Cresco Ltd

Tax planning for companies

Investments to save tax
- Capital expenditure.
- R&D expenditure.

Tax planning
- Optimum use of losses.
- Group structure.
- Maximising group corporation tax reliefs.

chapter 18

Value added tax

In this chapter

- Introduction.
- Types of supply.
- VAT registration.
- VAT groups registration.
- Deregistration.
- VAT returns.
- Output VAT.
- Input VAT.
- Special accounting schemes.
- Land and buildings.
- Partial exemption.
- Capital goods scheme.
- VAT administration.
- VAT penalties.

Value added tax

Exam focus

VAT can be examined in the context of companies or an unincorporated business.

The new topics introduced at ATX are popular topics, but retention of TX knowledge is also essential as all areas can be tested.

Introduction

- VAT is an indirect tax charged on consumer spending.
- VAT is charged on:
  - a taxable supply
  - by a taxable person
  - in the UK
  - in the course or furtherance of a business.
- Output tax: charged on sales.
- Input tax: incurred on purchases and expenses.

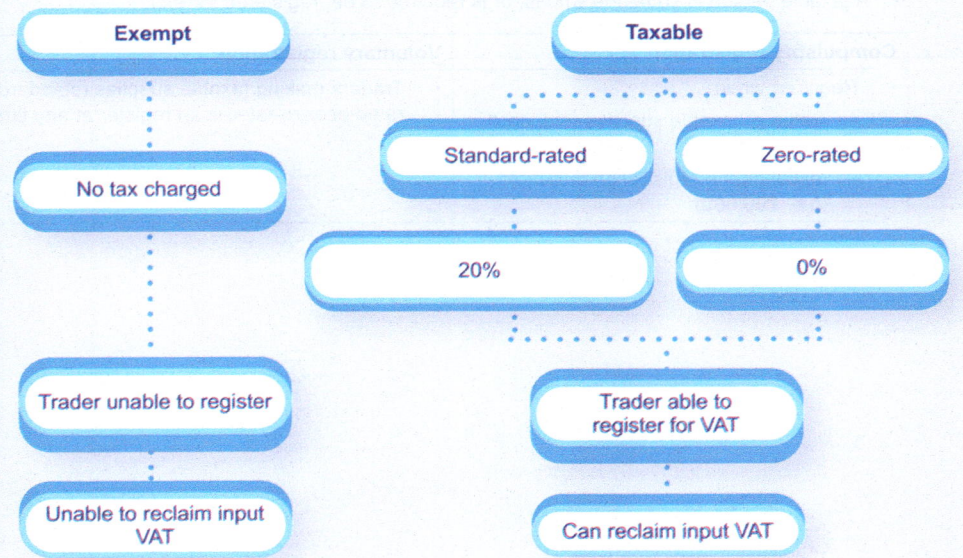

VAT registration

- A taxable person is someone who is, or is required to be, registered for VAT.

Compulsory registration	Voluntary registration

- Required when:
  – value of taxable supplies (standard or zero-rated)
  – exceeds the registration threshold (i.e. £90,000).
	- Traders making taxable supplies (standard rated or zero-rated) can register at any time.

Compulsory registration

Historic turnover test	Future test
• Taxable supplies in the last 12 months exceed £90,000. • Perform test at the end of each month.	• Taxable supplies in the next 30 days is expected to exceed £90,000. • Perform test constantly.
Inform HMRC:	
• Within 30 days of the end of the month in which the threshold is exceeded.	• By the end of the 30 day period in which the threshold is expected to be exceeded.
Registered from:	
• The first day of the second month after taxable supplies exceeded the threshold. • An agreed earlier date.	• From the start of the 30 day period.
If taxable supplies are wholly zero-rated there is an exemption from compulsory registration.	

Exam focus

Exam kit questions on this area:

Section A questions

- Sprint Ltd and Iron Ltd
- Ray, Shanira and Kelly

Section B questions

- Ash
- Dent Ltd

Value added tax

Voluntary registration

Advantages	Disadvantages

• Input tax recoverable.
• If making zero-rated supplies:
  – VAT returns will show VAT repayable
  – can register for monthly returns to aid cashflow.
• Avoids penalties for late registration.
• May give the impression of a more substantial business.
	• Output charged on sales:
	  – if make standard-rated supplies to customers who are not VAT registered will be an additional cost to them
	  – may affect competitiveness.
	• VAT administration burden.

Exam focus

Exam kit questions on this area:

Section A questions
- Olma and Hogan

Section B questions
- Dent Ltd
- Tomas and Ines
- Desiree

VAT Group registration

- Membership
  - voluntary
  - by any UK companies under common control
  - non-corporate entities may form a VAT group if they are the controller of a group of companies and have a UK trade.
- Consequences
  - Representative member responsible for accounting for VAT
  - No VAT on intra-group sales
  - Only one VAT return to prepare
  - All members jointly and severally liable for group VAT
  - Limits for cash accounting scheme applied to whole group
  - Other VAT schemes for small businesses not available.

Be prepared to explain whether or not a company should be included in a VAT group.

- Special consideration required for:
  - company making zero-rated supplies
    - exclude if in monthly repayment position to maintain cash flow advantage
  - companies making exempt supplies
    - inclusion in group will make the group partially exempt.

Exam focus

Exam kit questions on this area:

Section A questions

- Jeg Ltd Group
- Sprint Ltd and Iron Ltd
- Hahn Ltd Group
- Plad Ltd and Quil Ltd

Deregistration

Compulsory deregistration	Voluntary deregistration
• When cease to make taxable supplies. Inform HMRC: • within 30 days of ceasing to make taxable supplies. Deregistered from: • date of cessation, or • an agreed earlier date.	• If value of expected taxable supplies in the next 12 months will not be > £88,000. • At any time when above test satisfied. • Date of request for deregistration, or • An agreed later date.

- Consequences of deregistration
  - Deemed to make a supply of business assets held at date when cease to be a taxable person (e.g. capital items, trading inventory).
  - Exclude items if no input tax reclaimed on them (e.g. cars purchased with private use).
  - No output charge if VAT on deemed supply is ≤ £1,000.

Exam focus

Exam kit questions on this area:

Section A questions
- Ziti

Section B questions
- Acryl Ltd and Cresco Ltd
- Enid

VAT returns

- Normally quarterly.
- If receive VAT repayments can elect for monthly returns.
- VAT payable
  = (Total output tax less total input tax).
- A businesses must:
  - file the return online, and
  - pay electronically,
  - within one month and seven days of the end of the VAT period.
- VAT-inclusive amounts:
  - VAT
    = Gross amount x 20/120 (or 1/6)
  - Net amount
    = Gross amount x 100/120 (or 5/6)

Output VAT

Value of supply

- Consideration in money:
  - Trader's VAT-exclusive selling price less the amount of any trade or bulk buy discounts offered.
- If a prompt payment discount is offered, VAT is charged on the amount received.
- Consideration not in money, or money and something other than money:
  - Open market value.
- Gifts of inventory and non-current assets
  - Replacement value.
- Certain gifts are not taxable supplies:
  - goods which cost ≤ £50 per customer, per year, and
  - any number of business samples, and
  - gifts of service (to employees or customers).
- Goods for own use
  - Replacement value if purchased for business purposes (no output VAT purchased for private purposes).

Relief for irrecoverable debts

- Relief available where:
  - output VAT in respect of an outstanding debt has been accounted for and paid by the supplier
  - the supplier has written the debt off in the accounts as irrecoverable
  - six months has elapsed since the debt was due for payment.
- Claim the relief as input VAT on the VAT return.
- Customers who have not paid for goods services within 6 months of the due date must repay the input tax they have previously claimed.

Transfer of a going concern (TOGC)

- Transfer of a business is not treated as a supply for VAT purposes, therefore:
  - no output VAT charged on assets transferred by seller
  - no input VAT recoverable by purchaser.
- Conditions (all must be satisfied):
  - business transferred as a going concern
  - no significant break in trading
  - to a taxable person (VAT registered or liable to become VAT registered)
  - same type of trade carried on after the transfer.
- A building on which an option to tax has been made cannot be part of the TOGC
  - unless the purchaser also opts to tax the building.
- Transferee may:
  - take over VAT registration of the transferor, but
  - also inherits the transferor's VAT liabilities.
- Where there is a transfer of a business which does not meet the VAT TOGC conditions:
  - VAT is payable on the individual assets transferred.

Exam focus

Exam kit questions on this area:

Section A questions

- Ziti
- Grand Ltd Group

Value added tax

Input VAT

- Conditions to reclaim input VAT:
  - Must be taxable person when incurred (exception = pre-registration VAT).
  - Supply must have been to the person making the claim.
  - Supply must be properly supported, normally by VAT invoice.
  - Goods/services must be used for business purposes.
- No distinction between capital and revenue expenditure.
  - Input VAT is recoverable on the purchase of capital assets as well as revenue expenditure.

Non-deductible VAT

- Business entertainment
  - includes hospitality of any kind (e.g. food, drink, accommodation)
  - excludes staff entertainment, and entertaining overseas customers.
- Cars
  - Purchase – only recoverable if used 100% for business or purchased for re-sale.
  - Leasing – if partly used for private purposes, only 50% of VAT on leasing charge recoverable.
  - Motor expenses – provided some business use, 100% recoverable.
  - If input VAT is not recovered on purchase, output VAT is not charged on the disposal.

- Fuel – Input tax 100% deductible even if private fuel provided

    Output VAT chargeable on:
    - fuel reimbursed in full
        - amount reimbursed.
    - not reimbursed in full
        - fuel scale charge (based on CO_2 emissions)
        - scale charge will be provided in examination.
- Private use
    - input VAT cannot be claimed on goods or services not used for business purposes
    - an apportionment is made for partial private use.
- Goods for own use
    - input VAT recoverable if purchased for business purposes (not recoverable if purchased for private purposes).

Key Point

Where VAT is not recoverable on capital expenditure (e.g. purchase of a car) capital allowances are claimed on the VAT-inclusive cost.

Pre-registration input VAT

Conditions to reclaim input VAT:

Goods	Services
- Acquired in the 4 years before registration, and - Still held at date of registration	- Supplied in the 6 months before registration

Exam focus

Exam kit questions on this area:

Section A questions
- Joe and Fiona
- Ray, Shanira and Kelly

Value added tax

Special accounting schemes

- Three special schemes aimed at small businesses.

Cash accounting scheme

Operation	Conditions	Advantages
• VAT accounted for on cash payments and cash receipts	• Taxable turnover ≤ £1,350,000 • VAT payments and returns must be up to date • Must leave the scheme if taxable turnover > £1,600,000	• Do not pay output tax until receive payment from customer • Provides automatic relief for irrecoverable debts

Exam focus

Exam kit questions on this area:

Section A questions

- Drench, Paprikash, Hail Ltd and Rain Ltd

Flat rate scheme

Operation	Conditions	Advantages
• Flat rate of VAT applied to total turnover (including exempt supplies and VAT) • Flat rate determined by trade sector • Flat rate only used to simplify preparation of VAT return – still need to issue tax invoices	• Taxable supplies for the next 12 months ≤ £150,000 • Businesses are eligible to stay in the scheme until their VAT-inclusive turnover exceeds £230,000	• Reduces administration – do not need to account for VAT on individual purchases • May reduce total VAT payable

Value added tax

Annual accounting scheme

Operation	Conditions	Advantages

• One VAT return prepared a year
• Return due:
2 months after end of annual VAT period
• Payments on account (POA):
  – 9 POA due in months 4 – 12
  – each POA is 10% of VAT for previous year
• Balancing payment due with the VAT return on same date
• New businesses base POA on estimated VAT liability
	• Taxable turnover ≤ £1,350,000
	• VAT payments and returns must be up to date
	• Must leave scheme if taxable turnover > £1,600,000
		• Reduces administration
		• Regular payments can help cashflow

Exam focus

Exam kit questions on this area:

Section A questions

- Hahn Ltd Group

Land and buildings

Types of supply

Supplies of land and buildings in the UK can be either be zero-rated, standard-rated or exempt.

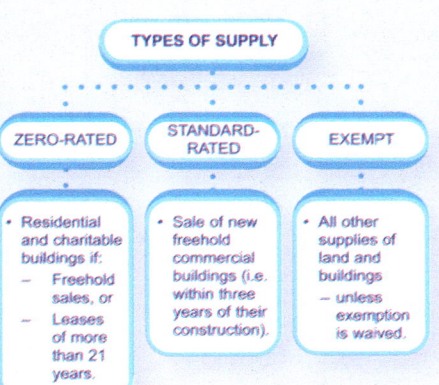

Opting to tax

A VAT registered vendor or lessor of a building can opt to waive the exemption of the building. This is usually referred to as 'opting to tax.'

Exam focus

Exam kit questions on this area:

Section A questions

- Hum Ltd Group
- Janus plc Group
- Ziti
- Grand Ltd Group
- Joe and Fiona

Section B questions

- Achiote Ltd
- Maria and Granada Ltd

Value added tax

OPTION TO TAX

CONDITIONS

- Election must be filed within 30 days of signing.
- Can be withdrawn within initial 6 month cooling off period or after 20 years otherwise irrevocable.
- Election cannot be made for a part of a building, although the election can be made separately for each property owned.

IMPACT

- Supply becomes a taxable supply.
- Input tax in respect of the building can be recovered.
- Future supplies of the building (e.g. sales or rents, must be standard-rated).
- New owners are not bound by a previous owner's election, except for transfers within a VAT group (later in this chapter).

Partial exemption

Traders who make both taxable and exempt supplies:

- only part of the input tax is recoverable.

Exam focus

Exam kit questions on this area:

Section B questions

- Spetz Ltd Group
- Nocturne Ltd

Methods of determining recoverable input tax

The standard method for determining the amount of recoverable input VAT is as follows:

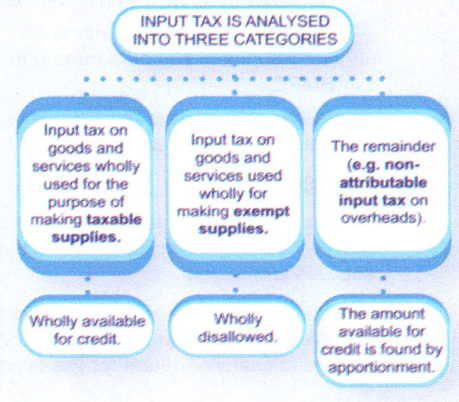

INPUT TAX IS ANALYSED INTO THREE CATEGORIES

- Input tax on goods and services wholly used for the purpose of making **taxable supplies**. → Wholly available for credit.
- Input tax on goods and services used wholly for making **exempt supplies**. → Wholly disallowed.
- The remainder (e.g. **non-attributable input tax** on overheads). → The amount available for credit is found by apportionment.

Value added tax

- Non-attributable input VAT reclaimable:

$$\frac{\text{Total taxable supplies (exc. VAT)}}{\text{Total supplies}} = \%$$

  - Exclude supplies of capital goods
  - Round % up to next whole number
  - Any other reasonable method of apportionment can be agreed with HMRC.
- Can either calculate the reclaimable % each quarter or can use last year's %.

Annual adjustment

- Recalculate recoverable % at the end of each accounting period based on actual supplies for the year.
- Any under or over-claim accounted for in first VAT return of next year, or can bring forward to final VAT return for this period.

De minimis limits

- All input tax (including that relating wholly or partly to exempt supplies) may be recovered if the business is below the de minimis limits.
- Three tests to check whether a business is de minimis:

  (1) **Total input tax ≤ £625 per month** on average, and
  Value of **exempt supplies ≤ 50%** of value of **total supplies**

  (2) **Total input tax less input tax directly attributable to taxable supplies ≤ £625 per month** on average, and
  Value of **exempt supplies ≤ 50%** of value of **total supplies**

  (3) **Input tax relating to exempt supplies ≤ £625 per month** on average, and
  Input tax relating to exempt supplies ≤ 50% of total input VAT

- Only need to satisfy one test.
- If business was de minimis last year:
  - can provisionally recover all VAT this year (unless input tax expected to be > £1 million).
- Status must be reviewed at end of the accounting period based on whole year.
- Annual adjustment made as above, if necessary.

Annual test

- The business can apply the de minimis tests once a year rather than every return period if:
  - the business was de minimis in the previous year, and
  - the annual test is applied consistently throughout the current year, and
  - the input VAT for the current year is not expected to exceed £1 million.
- This means that the business can provisionally recover all input VAT relating to exempt supplies in each return period without having to perform de minimis calculations.
- At the end of the accounting period, the de minimis status must be reviewed based on the year as a whole and an annual adjustment made if necessary.

Capital goods scheme

- Applies to partially exempt traders who spend large sums on land and buildings or computer equipment.
- Initial deduction of input tax is made in the ordinary way and then reviewed over a set adjustment period.

Value added tax

- Assets covered by the scheme:

Item	Value	Adjustment period
Land and buildings	£250,000 or more	10 years (5 years where subject to a lease of less than 10 years at acquisition)
Computers and computer equipment	£50,000 or more	5 years

A trader making say 70% taxable supplies and 30% exempt supplies:

- can initially reclaim 70% of the input VAT charged in respect of a building
- adjustments are made over the next 10 (or 5) years if the proportion of exempt supplies changes.

The annual adjustment is:

$$\frac{\text{Original input tax}}{10 \text{ or } 5 \text{ years}} \times (\text{\% now} - \text{\% in the original year})$$

Disposal of asset in adjustment period

- normal annual adjustment
- further adjustment

if disposal:	for remainder of adjustment period assume
taxable	100% taxable use
exempt	0% taxable use

Exam focus

Exam kit questions on this area:

Section A questions
- Janus plc Group
- Jake

Section B questions
- Hyssop Ltd
- Rosa
- Yaqui

VAT administration

VAT records

- Must keep records of all goods/services received and supplied, sufficient to allow the return to be completed and allow HMRC to check the return.
- Retain records for 6 years.
- Type of records to retain:
  - copies of VAT invoices issued
  - record of outputs (e.g. sales day book)
  - evidence to support recovery of input tax
  - VAT account.

VAT penalties

- **Standard penalties** apply in the same way for income tax, CGT, corporation tax and VAT.
- Depends on the behaviour of the taxpayer (Chapter 10).
- Errors in VAT returns can give rise to
  - Interest, and
  - Standard penalty for the submission of an incorrect VAT return.

Specific penalties relating to VAT

- Late filing penalties
- Late payment penalties.

Value added tax

Late filing penalties

A points-based system applies for late submission of VAT returns.

- Each time a quarterly VAT return is submitted late, the taxpayer receives one penalty point.
- Once the taxpayer reaches the threshold of **four penalty points**, a **£200 penalty** is charged.
- Every subsequent late VAT return will also incur a £200 penalty, but the points total will not increase further.
- While the taxpayer is below the penalty points threshold, each penalty point expires after two years.
- However, once the threshold has been reached, penalty points do not expire. Instead, the taxpayer must submit all VAT returns on time for a 12-month period (i.e. four quarterly returns) to reset the points to zero.

Late payment penalty

Days after payment due date	Penalty
Up to 15 days	None
16 to 30	2%
Day 31	4% plus daily penalty at an annual rate of 4%

The penalties for late submission and late payment can be cancelled if the taxpayer has a reasonable excuse.

Error on VAT returns

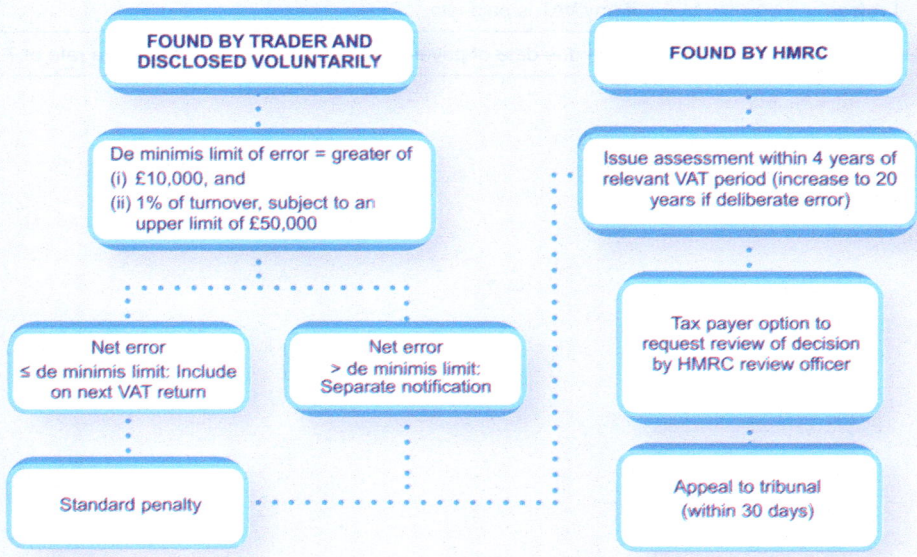

Value added tax

Late payment interest

Arises	• If any VAT is paid late.
Charged	• From due date of payment to actual date of payment at a rate of 7.75%

Index

Index

A

Additional rate band 188
Additional tax on lifetime transfers as a result of donor's death 121
Adjusted income 224
Adjusted total income 190, 299
Advantage of lifetime gifts 142
Agricultural property relief 127, 132
AIA 11, 277
Allowable employment expenses 201
AMAP 201, 202, 204
Amendments 22
Amendments to the return 176
ANI 191
Annual accounting scheme 340
Annual adjustment 344
Annual allowance 223
Annual exempt amount 70
Annual exemption 127, 128
Annual Investment Allowance 277
Annual party 202

Appeals 184
Approved mileage allowance payments 204
APs 2
Arising basis 235
Asset damaged 78
Assets lost or destroyed 77
Assignment of leases 73, 76
Associated companies 19, 20, 21, 33
Augmented profits 21
Automatic non-UK residency tests 231
Automatic UK residency tests 231
Average method 208

B

Badges of trade 267
Balancing adjustments 279
Balancing allowance 279
Balancing charge 279
Balancing payment 177
Baseline amount 135
Basic charge 206
Basic rate band 188

Basis of assessment 285
Beneficial loans 208
Benefits 202
Benefits on retirement 226
Bonus issues 86
BPR 129
Branch 54
Branch exemption election 57
Business asset disposal relief 94, 95, 104
Business property relief 127, 129
Business records 176
Business vehicle 309

C

Capital allowances 11, 275, 288
Capital allowances available for cars 280
Capital gains group 33, 41
Capital gains tax planning 253
Capital goods scheme 345
Capital losses 29, 79, 91
Car benefit 205
Carry back relief 24
Carry forward relief 24
Cash basis 269
Cash basis for property income 195
Cash earnings 216
Cash ISA 194
Cessation of business 288
CFCs 59
CGT computation 70
Chargeable assets 69
Chargeable disposals 69
Chargeable gain computation 71
Chargeable Lifetime Transfers 117
Chargeable persons 69
Charitable legacies 135
Chattels 73, 75
Class 1A NIC 217
Class 1 (employee) 216
Class 1 (employer's) 217
Class 4 (NIC) 287
Close companies 316
Close investment company 318
CLTs 117

Company residence 52
Compliance checks 22, 183
Compulsory deregistration 332
Compulsory registration 329
Conflicts of interest 158
Connected persons 80
Consortium 34
Consortium relief 40
Controlled foreign companies 59
Corporation tax payable 3
CSOP 212
Current year relief 24

D

Dealing with HMRC 159
Death estate 123, 133
Debt versus Equity 306
Deed of variation 135, 137
Deemed domicile for income tax and capital gains tax 229
Deemed domicile for inheritance tax 248
Deemed occupation 101
Degrouping charge 41
De minimis limits 344
Depreciating assets 105
Deregistration 332
Determination of tax 176
Diminution in value 118, 124
Disadvantages of lifetime gifts 142
Discovery assessments 183
Discretionary trust 147
Dishonest conduct of tax agents 162
Dividend nil rate band 189
Dividends income 193
Domicile 229
Double tax relief (CGT) 247
Double tax relief (IHT) 127, 136, 250
Double tax relief (income tax) 239
Due dates of payment (IHT) 123

Index

E

EIS 166, 168, 192, 255
EIS reinvestment relief 94, 171
EMI 97, 212
Employee class 1 216
Employer's class 1 217
Employment allowance 216, 217
Employment income 200
Employment versus self-employment 258
Error on VAT returns 349
Exempt assets (CGT) 69
Exempt benefits 202
Exempt disposals 69
Exempt income 194
Exemptions to CFC charge 60
Exempt legacies 134
Exempt supply 327
Ex-gratia payments 215
Exit charge 151
Expensive accommodation charge 206
Extracting profits from a business 312

F

Fall in value relief 128
Filing date (companies) 19
Filing dates (individuals) 175
Financing non-current assets 308
First year allowances 278
Flat rate expenses 273
Flat rate scheme 339
Free shares 213
Fuel scale charge 337
Full expensing 13
Furnished holiday lettings 197
Future test 329
FYA 278

Index

G

General anti-abuse rule 161
Gift holdover relief 94, 197
Gift of assets 209
Gifts with reservation 134
Giving advice to clients 164
Goodwill 6
Group payment arrangements 20
Group relief 33, 37, 46

H

Higher rate band 188
Hire purchase 308
Historic turnover test 329

I

IHT and CGT on sales/gifts 141
IHT computations 118
IIP trust 147, 150
Income tax computation 188
Income tax payable 189
Income tax planning 253
Incorporation relief 94, 292
Individual savings accounts 194
Inheritance tax 116
Inheritance tax planning 254
Input VAT 326, 336
Inspection powers 184
Intangibles 6
Intangibles rollover relief 6
Integral features 281
Interest received gross 193
Interest received net 193
Investment products 166
Investors' relief 99
IR35 319
ISAs 194

J

Job-related accommodation 206, 207
Joint income 193

K

Key investment products 166

L

Large companies 21
Late filing of corporation tax return 23
Late filing penalties (individuals) 181
Late payment interest 20, 178
Late payment penalties (individuals) 182
Legacies to charity 135
Letting relief 94
Life assurance 126
Life tenant 147
Lifetime gifts 117
Lifetime giving versus legacies on death 264
Lifetime tax 120
Liquidation 90, 322
Living accommodation 206
Living expenses 206
Loan relationship deficits 29
Loan relationships 5
Location of assets 249
Long term finance 306
Losses on unquoted shares 91
Lump sum payments 215

M

Market value of quoted shares 84
Marriage Allowance 191
Marriage exemption 127
Married couples and civil partners 82, 138, 193
Married couples/civil partners tax planning 261
Matching rules 84
Matching rules – individuals 84
Matching shares 213
Maximum deduction from total income 190, 299
Medical treatment 202
Mergers 88
Money laundering regulations 160

Index

N

National Insurance Contributions 216
New clients 156
Nil rate bands 119
Non-cash vouchers 202
Non-savings income 193
Non-trading losses 29
Non-UK residents and UK non-residential property disposals 246
Non-UK residents and UK residential property disposals 246
Non-wasting chattels 75
Normal expenditure out of income 127
Notification of chargeability 175
NS&I savings certificates 194

O

Occupational Pension Plan 221
Official rate of interest 208
Opening years relief 297
Option to tax 342

Output VAT 326, 334
Overseas aspects of VAT 63
Overseas branch 54
Overseas subsidiary 54

P

Paper for paper 88, 89
Parental dispositions 193
Part disposals 73, 74
Partial exemption 343
Partnerships 302
Partnership shares 213
Payment by instalments (IHT) 137
Payment date (companies) 19
Payment dates (individuals) 177
Payments on account 177
Payroll deduction scheme 201
Pension income 226
Pensions 220
Personal allowance 190
Personal financial management 165
Personal Pension Plan 221

Personal service company 319
Personal trading company 96
PETs 117
Precise method 208
Pre-entry capital loss 43
Premium for granting short leases 196
Pre-registration input VAT 337
Principal charge 151
Private fuel 205
Private residence relief (PRR) 100
Private use assets 283
Professional Code of Ethics 156
Property income 195
Property income losses 29, 195
PRR 100
PRR for non-UK resident individuals 246
Publication of names of tax offenders 163
Purchase of own shares 322, 323

Q

QCBs 90
QCDs 4
Qualifying charitable donations 4
Quarterly instalments 19
Quick succession relief 127, 136

R

RDEC 8
Real estate investment trusts 198
Reallocation of gains 42
Records 20, 176
Reduction of PA 191
Redundancy payments 200, 215
Related 51% group companies 33, 36
Related property 124
Relevant business property 129, 130
Relevant earnings 222
Relevant property trust 150
Relief against chargeable gains 296
Relief against future trading profits 296

Relief against total income 296
Reliefs 190
Relocation expenses 202
Remittance basis 236, 242
Remittance basis charge 238, 243
Rent-a-room relief 197
Repayment interest 20, 178, 194
Replacement furniture relief 195
Research and development expenditure 7
Residence (company) 52
Residence (individuals) 230, 232
Residence nil rate band (RNRB) 119
Restriction of annual allowance 224
Restriction of carry forward of losses 28
Restrictive covenants 215
Rights issues 86
Rollover relief 42, 94, 102, 197

S

Sale of rights (nil paid) 87
Sale of shares or assets 46
Save As You Earn 194
Savings income 189, 193
Savings nil rate band 189
SAYE 194, 212
SDLT 112
SEIS 166, 168, 192, 255
SEIS reinvestment relief 94, 172
Self-assessment 19, 175, 304
Serious tax offenders 162
Share for share exchange 88
Share incentive plan 201
Share options 210
Share pool 10, 85
Share valuation rules (CGT) 84
Short life assets 282
Short term finance 307
SIP 201, 213
Skipping a generation 143

Index

Small gifts 127
Small part disposals 74
Small pool WDA 282
Sole trader versus company 309
Sources of finance 174
Special rate pool 281
Splitting tax year 232, 233
Stamp duty 112, 113
Stamp duty land tax 112, 113
Stamp duty reserve tax 112, 113
Standard penalties 23, 179, 347
Standard-rated 327
Status Determination Statement 320
Statutory redundancy pay 194, 215
Stocks and shares ISA 194
Structures and buildings allowances 16, 285
Subscriptions 201
Subsidised canteen 202
Substantial legacies to charity 135
Substantial shareholding exemption 9
Sufficient ties tests 231, 232
Supply of services 63

T

Takeovers 88, 89
Taper relief 122
Taxable benefits 202
Taxable total profits computation 3
Tax avoidance 161
Tax efficient expenditure 255
Tax efficient remuneration 256
Tax evasion 161
Tax free lump sum 226
Tax reducers 192
Tax Tribunals 185
Temporary absence abroad 245
Temporary workplace 201
Tenants in common 126
Terminal loss relief 28, 298
Termination payments 215
Threshold income 224
TOGC 335
Trading losses 24, 296
Trading loss pro forma 25

Index

Transfer of a going concern 335
Transfer of assets within group 41
Transfer of trade within a 75% group 48
Transfer of unused nil rate band 139
Transfer of value 124
Transfer pricing 49
Transition profits 286
Trust deed 146
Trustees 146
Trusts 146

U

Use of assets 209
Use of furniture 206

V

Valuation (IHT) 124
Valuation rules 84
Value of supply 334
Van benefit 205
VAT 326
VAT administration 347
VAT group registration 331
VAT on exports 63
VAT on imports 63
VAT penalties 347
VAT records 347
VAT registration 328
VCT 166, 168, 192, 194, 255
Voluntary deregistration 332
Voluntary registration 330

W

Wasting chattels 75
WDA 12, 278
Withdrawing investment 322
Workplace nurseries 202
Workplace parking 202
Writing down allowance 278

Z

Zero-rated 327